WITHDRAWN

THE QUETZAL IN FLIGHT

Quetzal, by Emanuel Paniagua.

THE QUETZAL IN FLIGHT

*Guatemalan Refugee Families
in the United States*

NORITA VLACH

Westport, Connecticut
London

Library of Congress Cataloging-in-Publication Data

Vlach, Norita.
    The Quetzal in flight : Guatemalan refugee families in the
United States / Norita Vlach.
    p. cm.
  Includes bibliographical references and index.
    ISBN 0-275-93979-0 (alk. paper)
    1. Guatemalan American families. I. Title.
  E184.G82V57   1992
  305.868'7281073—dc20   91-36410

British Library Cataloguing in Publication Data is available.

Library of Congress Catalog Card Number: 91-36410
ISBN: 0-275-93979-0

First published in 1992

Praeger Publishers, 88 Post Road West, Westport, CT 06881
An imprint of Greenwood Publishing Group, Inc.

Printed in the United States of America

The paper used in this book complies with the
Permanent Paper Standard issued by the National
Information Standards Organization (Z39.48-1984).

10 9 8 7 6 5 4 3 2 1

The author and publisher gratefully acknowledge Patricia Amlin for permission
to quote from *Popul Vuh: Creation Myth of the Maya*, an ethno-animated film
written, directed, and produced by Patricia Amlin, funded by the National
Endowment for the Humanities. © 1989.

To Bill

His enthusiasm, respect, humor, experience,
and love have made this research and its
writing possible.

To Tanya and Jacinta

You have taught me what it means to have a
strong and caring family.

When a man dies, people are afraid of his bones.
But his essence is not lost.
It remains whole and lives on
in his sons and daughters.

—Popol Vuh

CONTENTS

FIGURES AND TABLES

FIGURES

TABLES

PREFACE

The quetzal is a brilliantly colored tropical bird of Central America that, according to legend, lost its voice following the Spanish conquest. It is Guatemala's national symbol of independence and pride. Environmentalists have decried both the wanton killing of this majestic bird for its plumage and the destruction of its rainforest home. But it is not only the birds and animals who are suffering an ecological disaster. The people of Guatemala are also in flight. This book dramatizes the story of a new set of immigrants—refugees, in fact—who are now living here in the United States.

The image of the quetzal serves as a backdrop to this book and to my own upbringing as a Guatemalan-American. Born and raised in Oakland, California, I was aware of having an ethnic tinge. Although my "rich" paternal grandmother (she owned her own home in which we lived downstairs) was German, she was two generations away from Germany, she did not speak German, and she was stern and a little cold. She was not my favorite grandmother. My other grandmother was the "poor" one. She spoke English with a thick accent, wrote and spelled English atrociously, cooked *chilaquiles* and had a marimba in her front room. She walked around with a book on her head ("for good posture"), stood on her head every morning ("it's good for the blood"), and dabbled in a number of offbeat religious sects. She was funny and warm; she taught me Spanish when I was very small, including pronunciation rhymes so that I would speak correctly:

Rrrre con rrre cigarro,
Rrrre con rrre barril,

Qué rápido corren los carros
Del ferrocarril..!

She also showed me newspaper clippings about my famous grandfather, a composer and pianist (he once played in Carnegie Hall, she told me). The pride was mixed with bitterness, though. He had deserted her early in the marriage, shortly after my mother's birth. He had had two other wives and several other children, but these unpleasant details weren't mentioned.

My mother didn't talk to me about my grandfather. She did none of those things that my grandmother did. We spoke English in our home, I grew up an "American," and my irreverent Guatemalan-American uncle referred to the quetzal as "a cockroach in drag!" When I reached my teenage years we moved to the suburbs. One thing about my home life, though: my mother collected refugees. Her close friends were some Latina women and the wives of my father's high school and college friends, but she was closest to two European women and their families who were refugees from World War II. My best friends were their children.

Much later, early in my social work career (1970), I decided to take a sabbatical, a leisurely motor trip to Guatemala. My grandmother had gone occasionally, and she had even spoken as an honored guest at the Presbyterian girls' high school from which she graduated many years earlier. But when I approached her about my plans to try to locate relatives still living in Guatemala, she discouraged me, saying that there were no living relatives. Undaunted, when I made the trip I looked up the Music Conservatory in Guatemala City where I knew my grandfather had taught. His picture appeared prominently at the entrance, and I was told that his son (my mother's half-brother and my uncle) also taught there. We had a very exciting meeting, and I felt doors opening to me. During this visit I was fascinated by the lush and varied countryside and by the friendly people. I was also disturbed by the fascist overlay and extreme tension regarding guerrilla activity in the eastern and Petén (northern rainforest) areas.

When I returned home, I began working as a community mental health social worker in Latino communities. I was struck by the schism in my own family history—between the immigrant family and the relatives who chose to stay behind. I began to formulate a strong interest in the phenomenon of migration and its effect on family life, which is the subject of this book.

In 1978 the Nicaraguan revolution again shook me into reexamining power and politics in Guatemala. I began saving newspaper clippings. Nicaragua. El Salvador. Guatemala. Honduras. All were being drawn into polemics vis-à-vis the United States and Cuba. In the late winter of 1981 we received word from my uncle and his family that they had moved suddenly to Mexico because of the "worsening political climate and economy."

I began my work on a study of Guatemalan immigrant/refugee families in 1982 while headlines reported the bloody war against the populace raging in El Salvador and the streams of Salvadoran refugees making their way across the U.S. border.

I was working in the wake of a fresh coup by Ríos Montt, a prominent military politician who also was a member of an actively proselytizing American evangelical sect. I found it curious that although American anthropology had had an historical fascination with Guatemala and its traditional Indian population; studies of its present-day immigrants and refugees were long overdue.

In my perusal of research on immigration and refugeeism, I find no work that has examined the Guatemalan immigrant family in the United States as, for example, Oscar Lewis has examined on Mexican and Puerto Rican families (Lewis 1959; 1961; 1966). There is, in fact, nothing comparable on any Central American country of origin. Most research lumps Latinos into a generic category of "Hispanic" or "Spanish-speaking" or focuses on Chicanos/Mexicanos, Puerto Ricans, or Cubans. From a comparative perspective it makes sense to isolate some of the peculiarities of the uniquely Guatemalan experience so that idiosyncratic features may be recognized and better understood and the more universal or pan-Latino phenomena may stand out more clearly.

This book has two objectives: (1) examination of motives for migration to the United States of Guatemalan families with teenagers, and (2) exploration of the processes of psychological change and adaptation that take place within these families during the early period of resettlement. To these ends, I examined the lives of six families. All were recent arrivals at the time of the study and all were families with an adolescent child.

The book is divided into three parts. Chapter 1 provides a theoretical framework for understanding migration, specifically the social, structural, and psychological context. In Chapter 2, I present the Guatemalan setting. The six families, introduced with pseudonyms, tell the stories of their origins, decisions to move, journeys, and settling-in. Methods included are participant observation, a set of semi-structured interviews, and two family evaluation tests, the Family Environment Scale and the Family Adaptability and Cohesion Scale. The findings are reported in case study fashion. (A more detailed explanation of the methodology including family testing instruments may be found in Appendix 2, while a mini-ethnography of the Guatemalan-American community in the San Francisco Bay Area is detailed in Appendix 1.)

In Chapter 3, I analyze various features of the Guatemalan immigrant experience. The families that were studied illustrate the effects of Guatemalan national upheaval in their decisions to come to the United States. Those families with the most stressful lives present a profile of characteristic adaptation and coping—centrifugal, or a pulling apart. The church emerges as an important institution in helping families cope. Certain family cultural styles and themes are drawn, and marital conflict is examined as a symbolic parallel to the civil war at home.

ACKNOWLEDGMENTS

Boundless appreciation to my dear mother and father. My mother, Marina Paniagua aroused my interest in Guatemala and in my own heritage. My father, William Jones, spent many hours typing and printing the original drafts of this manuscript. Their support and encouragement have been invaluable to me.

A number of other individuals have been of great help to me in the creation of this book. Margaret Clark shepherded me through the writing process with sensitivity and grace. Her thorough reading of the material made her suggestions and criticisms most pertinent. Stanley Brandes's and Carlos Sluzki's invigorating support were also a great boon to me. The art work was beautifully done by my cousin Emanuel Paniagua, and the final drafts of the document were prepared by Marilyn Vella.

Finally, I would like to thank the many individuals and families who opened their homes and their hearts to me and gave me the benefit of their counsel, wisdom, and experience. And I am truly grateful to my uncle, aunt, and cousins, Guatemalan refugees themselves, who taught me another reality as well as things I did not know about myself.

INTRODUCTION

It is a cool spring morning. I am seated in a small cubicle in an office on the main floor of Hospitality High School. I am told to wait just a few minutes. Mr. Balderama, the school counselor, finally appears. He is accompanied by a smiling, thirteen-year-old freshman boy. "This is Gordon," he tells me. Then he excuses himself and I am left with Gordon, who sits down in the chair across from me. He is an alert youth with hair neatly combed back, shiny dark eyes, and neutral-looking pressed slacks and shirt. Yes, he enjoys school very much, and he is doing well in his classes. It has been one year since he came from Guatemala to San Francisco. Gordon carefully copies down my telephone number to give to his mother. He tells me that she will be sure to call me so that I can explain my work to her.

Three months later I am seated on the edge of a bed in a tiny room that Gordon shares with his mother and older brother in the San Francisco Mission District. It is my next to last interview with the family and Gordon is seated, slumped over on the bed across from me. He is dressed in overalls and he has a cold. Sniffling in between responses, he gives a much more forlorn and childlike impression than he did that first day in the school counselor's office. "Yes," he says, "I have nightmares. I am in a big crowd. They are all staring at me. They look mean. I am scared. They move in toward me. I see an opening. When I move to it, I see that it is a cliff. I only want to jump off of it. If I do, I know that there will be no more problems."

Who is Gordon? Is he the fresh-faced smiling "A" student, the marvel immigrant pioneering a new life for his family and a successful future? Or is he the sad-eyed boy ridden with fears and doubts? This study takes a new look at the Gordons who are slipping quietly into the United States, at their families, and perhaps their futures.

THE QUETZAL IN FLIGHT

MIGRATION AND THE GUATEMALAN FAMILY

UNDERSTANDING MIGRATION

Social and behavioral scientists commonly offer two main orientations to migration theory. The dominant perspective in the social sciences is the historical-structural perspective, which attempts to explain the migration of people in terms of economic and political forces that impel them to leave their homes for a new land. The orientation most popular with behavioral scientists emphasizes acculturation and the migration experience (phenomenology) in terms of coping and adaptation. The role of social networks in moving and in resettling is usually considered. In choosing the appropriate approach for this study, I found that both perspectives have advantages and disadvantages.

The most incisive current work in the historical-structural vein explains the movement of people as propelled by a dynamic transnational capitalist economy (Zolberg 1989). Contact between sending and receiving societies often involves initial physical coercion of a dominant state to a subordinate state. This is followed by economic inducement (labor recruitment) and cultural diffusion (Portes and Borocz 1989). Laborers from the rapidly growing Third World can earn high wages relative to what they can get at home. The catch is that they have to move near to the centers of capital, where living expenses are correspondingly higher.

This "new world order" is creating increasing dislocations in societies that are subordinate and peripheral to centers of multinational corporations. The process of penetration has made traditional subsistence strategies obsolete and has displaced large sectors of the workforce. The theory argues that a new dual economy with a scaled-down opportunity structure is being fashioned. It is global in nature, separate, and distinctly unequal. New centers of immigrant growth are part of a massive low-wage, service-oriented, racially segregated, and increasingly feminized job supply. Moreover, migrants are not contributing to the steady growth of developing countries (via investment and remittances); instead, a topsy-turvy process of de-development in Third World countries is now under way (Sassen-Koob 1984; Portes and Bach 1985).

Corresponding to these macroeconomic trends is the rise of a new nativism, a trend that exists worldwide. From western Europe to eastern Europe, throughout Asia and the United States, there is a wave of anti-immigrant feeling that finds a more sophisticated voice than that of previous generations. In the United States, its most common target has been the Latin American community and its most prominent organization is U.S. English. Although overt racism is not characteristic of this organization, its agenda is similar to the more blatant anti-foreigner sentiment that led to the exclusionary and restrictive immigration legislation of the earlier part of this century (Zolberg 1989; Daniels 1990; Portes and Rumbaut 1990).

In addition to the problem of unwelcome reception, the conditions of immigrant exodus have become increasingly highlighted as the era of refugeeism has taken hold. Numerous revolutions, civil wars, and instances of political violence maintained by military dictatorships have penetrated the hinterlands and have caught civilians unaware. These conditions have become endemic, contributing to the increased numbers of refugees throughout the world since the late 1970s. Estimates are that from 1978 to 1988 the ranks of refugees have swollen from 5–10 million to some 18.5 million. For the same period in Central America, it has been estimated that there were some 1.9 million internally displaced refugees and that over 600,000 unrecognized and hidden Central Americans entered the United States (United States Committee for Refugees 1989).

Although refugees are by no means a new phenomenon, the idea of the refugee is relatively new in the United States. The first federal legislation that set refugee policy (as opposed to immigrant policy) was the Displaced Persons Act of 1948 following World War II. Until very recent times, the primary scope of U.S. refugee legislation was designed in an atmosphere of Cold War rhetoric, which meant that only refugees from communism were to be accepted. The Refugee Act of 1980 meant to rectify this policy by using the more internationally accepted concept of refugee "any person who is outside any country of his nationality and is unable or unwilling to avail himself of the protection of that country because of persecution or a well founded fear of persecution" (Daniels 1990, p. 346). This legislation pointedly disregards the political ideology of the origin country. In practice, however, preference for political asylum has been granted almost exclusively to those fleeing communism. The law also excludes those who have left their homes due to violence and war unless they have been singled out as targets because of race, religion, nationality, social group membership, or political orientation. (Ferris 1987; Daniels 1990; Portes and Rumbaut 1990). Other macroeconomic forces are detailed in an excellent example of the historical-structural study—William Durham's *Scarcity and Survival in Central America* (1977). Here, the international economic marketplace and the inequitable system of land tenure in El Salvador are examined in terms of their effect on migration patterns in the area prior to the recent intensification of civil war. Similar forces operate in Guatemala, although (as we shall see) the caste stratification system and other unique historical-structural features produce a somewhat different migration and adaptation pattern there (Durham 1977; Smith 1984; Moors 1988). Other more comparative studies of the same genre find parallels in labor procurement mechanisms in California and South Africa based on particular governmental strategies of control that ensure a supply of undocumented and therefore cheap and docile labor (Burawoy 1976; West and Moore 1989).

The advantage of the historical-structural approach is that it paints with broad and bold strokes; it is the context of experience. Newer models even claim some predictive power given the history of the relationship between potentially receiving and sending societies, movements of capital, technology, and cultural imperialism (Portes and Borocz 1989). The disadvantage of this approach is its abstraction and generality. It cannot be applied to specific situations, nor can it explain why certain individuals, families, and cultural groups move and adapt in certain ways and others do not.

The acculturational/phenomenological approach takes the particularist perspective vis-à-vis adjustment to a new environment that often reflects the point of view of the migrants themselves. Its character and level of analysis are essentially different from that of the historical-structural approach.

A few decades ago, most studies focused on problems of disorganization and marginality (Redfield 1947; Lewis 1966). Now, however, the accent is on the migrant as an optimist who takes an active role in forging his or her own destiny. Current theorists describe migrants as making strategic decisions, as following middle-class values of the dominant society, and as utilizing and creating social networks to resolve problems (Perlman 1976; Jacob 1980; Balgopal 1988). Acculturation is viewed as involving the personal choice of the migrant (Hansen 1952; Clark et al. 1976; Padilla 1980). Such a shift in perspective offsets earlier notions that the acculturation process must be a linear phenomenon in which migrants are swept into isolation from old cultural and social connections, consequently paying a high psychological price for their "social disintegration" (Leighton et al. 1963).

In contrast to the generally cheerful view of migrants actively shaping their own futures, these same migration studies also point out that migration is often a matter of an opportunity presenting itself to dissatisfied individuals or groups who are vulnerable to poor social and economic conditions at home. Schreiber explains that migration is often precipitated by a family crisis (or life stage transition) such as a recent marriage, broken engagement, pregnancy or birth of a child, illness or death of a family member, marital troubles, or the need for a dowry for a daughter. Family members caught in the throes of working out survival strategies may well be unsure and confused about the meaning and motives of their migration (Schrieber 1972). In reality, most migrants seldom have the luxury of planning ahead. Instead, they maximize risky but strategic opportunities, often gaining the chance to emigrate into situations of continued financial insecurity and discriminatory policies and practices in the host country (Schreiber 1972; Guillet and Uzzell 1976).

This type of migration is generally experienced more intensely by refugees who have been forced to flee, often for their lives (Freeman 1989). However, it is important not to overstate the conceptual distinction between refugees and immigrants. Key variables in the level of difficulty faced seem be the degree of urgency, the involuntary nature of the move, and the host country's perceptions of the same. The actual urgency of need varies greatly among both refugees and immigrants; immigrant mobility is often unplanned, under little control of the migrant, and thus not really voluntary even if it may be primarily economic. The host country might choose not to confer refugee status on certain national groups who may, in fact, be fleeing for their lives for political reasons. This is said to be the case for many Guatemalans and, until recently, most Central Americans (Portes and Rumbaut 1990; Vernez 1991).

Research has described kin and social networks as resources that are vital to refugees and immigrants. Understanding how they work gives us insight into the origins, make up, direction, and persistence of migratory and adaptive behavior. Examples of such resources are migration "chains," churches, extended families, ethnic communities, occupational organizations, labor bosses, dyadic patronage relationships, lineages, fictive kin, and friendship groups. Particularly targeted to Central American refugees are new underground railroads that are connected to loose coalitions of churches and church-related groups (Golden and McConnell 1986). Conflicts and constraints may occur when social networks are extremely tight or at certain periods in the life cycle, especially during early adulthood and old age (Cohler and Lieberman 1980). In general, though, networks provide migrants the means to make the trip and a sense of solidarity and identity; they render an invaluable contribution to migrants' social, psychological, and economic adjustment (Arizpe 1975; Lomnitz 1977; Keefe et al. 1979, Kuo 1986, Shisana and Celentano 1987; Boyd 1989).

Taking advantage of available opportunities and resources, migrants and refugees are usually pictured as adapting quickly to new settings (Ferguson, B. 1984). Women of rural origins in particular acquire new access to salaried work outside the home. Ambitions flourish; migrant families that have been studied have expressed great hopes that the next generation will advance the family's socioeconomic status (Guillet and Uzzell 1976; Aronowitz 1984; Suarez-Orozco 1989).

These examples provide an overview of the kinds of results found in acculturational/phenomenological studies. The advantage of this orientation over the historical-structural approach is its focused perspective. It provides more practical everyday information about the concomitants of movement of ethnic and social groups. But there are dangers in this perspective, and it has many critics. For example, scholars who have taken the acculturational/phenomenological perspective have traditionally fallen into ethnocentric traps that "blame the victim" (Romano 1973). The results of such scholarship can be a profound disservice to immigrant and refugee peoples, as the eugenics period of exclusionary legislation in U.S. history bears witness. This is because the context (what is spelled out in the historical-structural view) is given only perfunctory acknowledgement or is ignored. Recently there has been a resurgence of interest in the acculturational/ phenomenological perspective in policy circles. An incisive explanation and stinging critique of its newfound popularity has been offered by Bach and Schraml:

Fostered by the great popularity of supply-side economics in general and coupled with the familiar restrictionist approach to immigration policy during recessions, interest in the individual characteristics of migrants has surged in both intellectual and policy circles. Human capital theorists, for example, have successfully reintroduced to the migration literature the long-abandoned theory of assimilation to explain the progress of low-wage migrant laborers to comparable status with their low income ethnic groups in the U.S. . . . With astonishing similarities to the generally denounced ethnocentrism of the immigration debates of 1911 and 1918 and the Dillingham Commission, this human capital assimilation theory has revived the analytical importance of values motivations and even the intelligence of recent immigrants. While political and economic crises grip the sending countries, the human capital approach comfortably advises that emigration is simply the response of the so-called best individuals trying to improve themselves. Consequently, despite deeply rooted methodological biases, the effect of this individualism has been profoundly theoretical, empirical and political. To draw the lines between human capital theory and historical-structural research at the extreme not only flatters the former with the status of a paradigm but essentially legitimizes the political positions it supports. (1982, pp. 322–323)

In essence, then, the problem of paradigm for the concept of immigration experience presents itself in this study. Immigration experience defined herein is the experience of undertaking a permanent or semi-permanent change of residence from one geographical area to another and across political boundaries. It also refers to a "symbolic range of meanings" (Geertz 1973, pp. 5, 17), including a phenomenological perspective on the reasons for leaving at that particular time in the migrants' lives. Because the focus of my research is on motives for migration, family ties, and coping and adaptation among resettled Guatemalans in the United States, the historical-structural perspective is not appropriate. Yet the acculturational/phenomenological orientation is too flawed to stand alone.

Two solutions are proposed. First, I have chosen to examine coping and adaptation from three different levels of analysis—as suggested by an excellent monograph exploring the migration of Indian women to Mexico City (Arizpe 1975). Arizpe asserts that the job of the anthropologist is to describe the relationship between the personal experience of the migrant and the macrostructural order. Accordingly, the three levels of analysis are (1) salient historical-structural conditions of migration; (2) immediate and precipitating causes and circumstances: the "push" and "pull"; and (3) personal and family reasons for emigration. When all three levels are elucidated, their relationships can better be teased out.

Second, I have chosen the Guatemalan family rather than the individual migrant as the basic unit of my study. When the family is examined as an interacting system, it is possible to get a broader view of Guatemalan-American history and social structure. At the same time, families are functioning and dynamic units that cope and adapt throughout the migration process in complex and nonlinear ways (Sluzki 1973). Another reason that a family focus is critical concerns the role of women in contemporary migration. The feminization of the migrant labor force and the central place of the woman in household and family life are common themes in migration research. Since families either migrate together or conduct individual reconnaissance with the expectation that other family members will follow, a large portion of the migration flow turns out to be family-based. Thus, the family unit is a powerful entry point to the inner workings of what is most vital in immigrant life (Harbison 1981; Bach and Schraml 1982; Wood 1982; Boyd 1989; Rumbaut 1989).

COPING AND THE LATINO FAMILY CULTURE

The experience of migration has rarely been examined from the perspective of the family unit.[1] Most research in the migration field does not actually specify an association between migration and family processes. Theoretical and clinical work in the field of family processes and dynamics, however, has mushroomed in the past two decades as a consequence of the development of the family therapy movement.

The most influential paradigm has been attributed to the anthropologist Gregory Bateson; it is the family systems orientation. In this orientation the family is seen as an interactional system that operates cybernetically. That is, any change in one family member affects the other members and the group as a whole in a chain of circular causality. Thus, the family (usually nuclear) is the basic unit of study, but it is not seen merely as the sum of its individual members or even of a series of dyadic relationships. Rather, the functional pattern connecting all family transactions is studied, and there is an emphasis on homeostasis, stability, and continuity. In this paradigm, all families have certain normative rules based on family sociocultural values. These rules are operationalized in a sequence of patterned actions, reactions, and consequences that are regularly repeated by individual family members and by family subsystems. The behavioral sequences reinforce each family's idiosyncratic structure and organization and the way in which family members communicate with each other. In such a homeostatic system, change comes as a result of a crisis related to the biological time clock (life cycle and developmental crises, illness, birth, and death) and to shifts in the environment or the context in which the family finds itself. At these times, rules may be changed, communication patterns may be altered, and the organization and structure of the family may be renegotiated. Migration is one of those events in which the family homeostasis may be changed (Walsh 1982).

In general, the family systems orientation examines micro-events in a family and its institutional/network context; it proposes certain explanatory concepts (e.g., underorganized family, Aponte 1976; emotional cut-off, Bowen 1978; protection, Madanes 1981) that lend themselves more easily to clinical intervention. However, the approach is usually cross-sectional. There is rarely a vision for the future, and the process of change over time (inclusive of family of origin and culture of origin) is not evaluated in any sustained fashion.

Narrative and developmental approaches, however, offer the researcher a way to explore the family of origin, its history, and changes in its role and structure. These approaches have a more mythic and visionary quality. They are more in tune with symbolic-interactionist theories and a phenomenological-existential, less mechanistic approach to meaning (Goody 1958; Steinglass 1978; Walsh 1982; Sarbin 1986; Falicov 1988; Freeman 1989; Howard 1991).

Although both systems and developmental/narrative family approaches are used in this study to explore the experience of immigrant families, the primary model of analysis is derived from research on adaptive coping strategies. Adaptive coping strategies are the solutions that families and family members find to deal with problems, situations, and events as they occur. They may be inferred through observation of family behavior as it occurs during a stressful time. The two categories of coping strategy are cognitive and behavioral.

Research on family-based adaptive coping strategies derives primarily from the major works of Angell (1936) and Hill (1949). Angell examined families coping with the stress of unemployment during the Great Depression of the 1930s. Hill studied family separation and reunion during World War II. Hill developed a model of family processes of coping under stress that provides a strong basis for analyzing the migration experience for resettled Guatemalan families. It is the ABCX (processual) model of family stress and coping. In essence, A is the stress event or hardship. It interacts with B, the resources available, and C, how the family defines or perceives the stress event or hardship. The result is X, the family experience, which goes through phases of adjustment (McCubbin and Figley 1983).

The stress event or hardship (A) may be normative, that is, related to universal life cycle events (in this study, adolescence), or it may be non-normative, related to unexpected crises such as wars, natural disasters, or illness (in this study, migration). Usually, non-normative stressors have a more intense impact than normative ones. There can also be the situation of stressors occurring on top of other stressors; families may not have the resources to deal with more than one or two stressors at a time. A particular type of stress event that is "beyond the normal range of human experience" and is said to be traumatic has been the source of the much-researched and much-discussed psychiatric diagnosis "post-traumatic stress disorder" (American Psychological

Association 1987, pp. 247-251; van der Kolk 1987). How such traumatic stress impacts families has been the subject of current research as well (Figley 1989).

Resources (B) may be personal attributes (such as ability to speak English, coping techniques, health, access to money, or other social-structural characteristics relevant in a given context). They may be technological resources (such as telephones and access to jet travel), which lessen the sense of isolation many migrants feel. They may relate to strengths or limitations in the family system (such as close positive bonding of members, clear communication, or flexibility of structure and roles).

Family perception of the hardship (C) is virtually the same as the cognitive coping strategies that it utilizes. In one study, *Ain't No Big Thing: Coping Strategies in a Hawaiian-American Community*, migrants were found to minimize the impact of a stressful event in order to better cope with the overwhelming stimuli (Howard 1974). Migrants may also see the stressful event as a resource from which they draw strength for growth, transformation, and creativity (Walsh 1982). These perceptions vary from family member to family member, so it is important to determine whose perceptions take precedence vis-à-vis the family mythology; the amount of incongruity and discrepancy of point of view has systemic effects upon the family as well (McCubbin et al. 1980; Figley 1989).

Finally, the family experience (X) derives from the interaction of A, B, and C. It is difficult to make a judgment on "outcome" because the individual, family, and societal perspectives may differ, and because the family experience may shift and change over time. Hill sees three main phases of family adjustment to crisis: (1) disorganization, (2) recovery, and (3) a new level of reorganization (Hill 1949). Sluzki aptly ties his model of phases of migration (based on the family unit and family systems perspective) to physiology, experimental psychology, and the stress curve. He breaks down the process of migration into five steps: (1) preparation, (2) act of migration, (3) period of overcompensation, (4) period of decompensation, and (5) transgenerational phenomena (Sluzki 1979). For a time, he says, the migrating family mobilizes all of its resources in a particularly energized fashion. This period of overcompensation may be analogous to what has also been termed "psychic numbing" at the intrapsychic level (Lifton 1967). But this coping strategy gives way to a crisis period of decompensation in which identity conflicts take place and the stage is set for family rules to change, communication patterns to alter, and the organization and structure of the family to be renegotiated. If these issues are not resolved satisfactorily at this time, the family carries them as excess baggage and they may recapitulate as the children grow to adulthood, or even in succeeding generations.

The many ways in which Latino families adapt to the migration experience are linked to culture. I concur with Geertz's description of culture as an abstract "web of significance" or "socially established structure of meaning" that functions homeostatically to provide ready-made solutions to relationship issues between individuals, social systems, and their physical context (Geertz 1973, pp. 5, 17). Anthropologists have used this level of abstraction to compare the beliefs and values of a vast array of societies.

The modern Latino cultural web is based on indigenous ideas of harmony and balance in nature and in community relations. It is manifested today in the Spanish language and in reliance on social relationships that are personalistic and interdependent. There is also an emphasis on respect for authority,[2] hierarchical rank, and cooperative (within the family) rather than competitive styles of social interaction. Church leadership is also highly respected, and Catholic religious beliefs predominate.

For Latinos, the family is the most important social group. It is of greater significance than either the individual or extra-familial social units. Ties of loyalty, obligation, and social support go beyond the nuclear unit and encompass extended members, diluting the force of family hierarchical structure (patriarchal with strict rules vis-à-vis the children) and sex-role segregation (father as provider, mother as nurturer). This is the overly reified cultural ideal (Bernal and Flores-Ortiz 1982).

This level of analysis is, however, unwieldy and stereotypic when it is used to examine particular groups of people in their day-to-day lives. There are too many geographic, historical-structural, socioeconomic, interactive, and other variations. For the purposes of this study, the concept of family culture is the notion that best describes and operationalizes how specific families integrate their sociocultural values into a unique family style.

Since this study focuses on immigrant families from a particular country, a number of other variables must also be considered. Guatemalan national culture derives from shared traditions. This common national history contains numerous contradictions and conflicts. These include ethnic, racial, sexual, political, religious, economic, regional, and urban-rural tensions.

Family culture expresses itself through normative family rules of behavior at a particular stage in the life cycle. These rules are the commonly perceived assumptions as to how family members should conduct themselves. In terms of adolescence, some important issues involve autonomy and cohesion; communication patterns between parents and adolescents; perceptions of work and school-related activities; and minority, ethnic, and peer- and gender-related expectations and identifications.

Latino boys and girls are often expected to conform to certain work or educational plans of the parents. Immigrant families struggling through their period of overcompensation may have particularly high hopes for their sons. The boys may experience value conflicts with their parents such as the development of a *cholo* identity[3] or an inability to cope with the pressure of learning English and competing with Anglo students for scarce rewards. The usual concern of girls is who their future husband will be. Families who are well off may want to follow the customary *quinceñeros* ritual, which is more or less the equivalent of a coming-out party on the girls' fifteenth birthday. Latino families often admonish their daughters to date only within their ethnic group; however, this may not be possible for Guatemalan immigrant girls. (Numbers of Guatemalan immigrants are relatively small.) In any case, close supervision of dating and other mixed-gender activities may also create some value dissonance between parents and their acculturating, more independent-minded daughters (Cohen and Fernandez 1974; Falicov and Karrer 1980).

Many of the cultural expectations of the families in this study are challenged when they come into contact with U.S. society. How do families' identities, behavior, and coping styles shift and change with the stress of migration? What is the current thinking about the impact of this experience upon mental health?

MIGRANT MENTAL HEALTH

Uprooting and resettlement have profound effects on the psychological adjustment of Guatemalan families. Because there are so many types of migrations and circumstances surrounding the various kinds of movements, researchers have attempted to deal some order into the diversity of experiences. One way in which they have tried to control for the multiplicity of phenomena associated with migration has been to postulate the existence of intervening influences on the mental health of migrants. Such influences can be broken down into four major types: (1) migrant characteristics (demographic variables), (2) conditions of resettlement (ideology of the host society and how the migrants are treated), (3) circumstances of migration (specific events leading to the move), and (4) conditions in the society of origin.

Migrant characteristics have received the most extensive attention. Age, sex, marital status, stage in the family life cycle, previous health status, socioeconomic status, and sociocultural differences from hosts are some of the variables that have been cited as being predictive (singly or in various combinations) of a higher risk of psychiatric illness in migrants (Hollingshead and Redlich 1958; Srole et al. 1962; Schwab et al. 1979). But these variables are not useful out of context. In general, the epidemiological data confirm sociological expectations that the more social distance immigrants have from their hosts and from a sense of power in their lives, the greater the chance of psychological difficulty (Portes and Rumbaut 1990).

Resettlement conditions or the reception given to new arrivals are also said to influence migrant mental health. For example, crowded and inadequate housing of inner-city ghettoes, xenophobia, poor working conditions and schools, and restrictive immigration laws and policies are some of the stresses faced by migrants after arrival (Faris and Dunham 1939; Baucic 1976; Murphy 1977; Salcido 1979; Cohen 1979).

In this study of Guatemalan families, circumstances of migration and conditions in the society of origin are the key variables considered in the psychological experience of migrants to the United States.   In the migration literature generally, origin conditions are described only in a cursory way and only in comparison to the new setting. For example, Lomnitz (1977) postulates that migrants may feel more open to adopting a new home depending upon how alienated they felt in their society of origin and how much frustration they experienced there in achieving their goals. Migrants with stronger attachments to their home countries may feel guilty about leaving if the home communities regard migrants as traitors who have betrayed their countrymen, especially if home conditions are very bad (Murphy 1977).

The amount and quality of information available to migrants at home about the new setting may also be significant. For example, communities that have only limited knowledge about what to expect in the United States and at the same time promulgate a false picture of a new life as flowing with milk and honey, money growing on trees, and so forth, are bound to send out migrants who will suffer greatly with the shock of reality when they actually arrive. After migrant families arrive, different expectations from one generation to another may replicate these unrealistic expectations and may create family tension and conflict (Bourne 1975).

Specific events leading to the migration are usually seen as the circumstances that identify the individual or family as either a voluntary or involuntary (i.e., refugee) newcomer. Acculturative stress has been described as greater for native peoples (those who are subdued by a colonizing society) and for refugees, with voluntary migrants suffering to a lesser degree (Berry et al. 1987). (African-Americans originally brought to America as slaves are a special case and are not included in this analysis.) Developments in the behavioral sciences in the areas of stressful life events, developmental psychology, and war trauma have contributed to this new body of research. Many current studies are finding post-traumatic stress and related symptomatology to be wide-spread among refugees (Aron 1986; Boehnlein 1987) and even among immigrants and family members affected only indirectly by warfare or traumatic incidents (Arroyo and Eth 1985; Figley 1989; Salgado de Snyder et al. 1990).

Migration as a form of rapid social change leads to dissonance *changes* between migrant culture and host demands, demoralization, loss of status, and an increase in stress-related illness (Brody 1969; Muller 1976; Cohen 1979). Acculturative distress is difficult to assess among im-migrants due to culturally defined "emic" concepts of health and illness that do not fit the standard diagnostic nomenclature of western mental illness (Rogler et al. 1991). For Latinos, especially relevant are *nervios* (tension, stress), *susto* (anxiety, depression, literally soul loss), and *ataques* (attacks of uncontrollably strong emotions). According to some Latino folk healers (*curanderos*), healing of psychic trauma may involve the need to *deshecharse* or *desahogarse* (ventilate) soon after a traumatic event has occurred. This is to prevent psychological difficulties in the future (Argüello 1990). Others may use religious rituals (Day of Esqui-pulas in Guatemala or "speaking in tongues" among evangelicals) to provide an expressive venue. Some investigators have suggested that a stress curve operates over time for migrants; it shows emotional swings from elation to symptomatology and family conflict to recovery with variations based on social class of origin, conditions of leavetaking, and family role taking (Sluzki 1979; Rumbaut 1989).

A pragmatic nonideological coping strategy is often found to be useful, especially early in the migration process. Superficial identification with the manners and mores of the host (or cultural aggressor) is another common style of coping. Migrants may compartmentalize[4] and thus control the pain of loss through "psychic numbing" (Bernard et al. 1965; Lifton 1967). Migrants using this coping strategy may have difficulty in explaining inconsistencies in their opinions, feelings, and behavior (Lifton 1967; Moos and Moos 1976; Cohen 1979).

On the positive pole, psychic numbing may be seen as an important adaptive coping strategy in that it blocks out an overwhelming amount of external stimuli. Furthermore, the experience of migration may be "muscle-building," "immunizing"; it may "increase resistance resources" (Antonovsky 1971, p. 1578). In some circumstances, the process of migration may build a sort of generic competence; it may train people how to cope with change through a diverse of adaptive experiences. Mastery of such experiences is said to bring about a "personal integration on a higher level" (Hull 1979, p. 28).

In sum, successful psychological coping strategies for migrants appear to require a skillful balancing act. On the one hand, the migrant needs to block out old values and memories and build for the future. On the other hand, there is a strong pull to link the present with the past. Many people see immigrants who move voluntarily as being more future-oriented than refugees who are forced to break ties with their home country and who hold on tenaciously to memories of significant past experiences. While U.S. hosts tend to be more accepting of migrants who accept the assimilationist myth of the melting pot, clinicians have argued that the mental health of the migrant is more secure when there is some link to the past.

Clinical evidence has repeatedly emphasized the need for the expression of symbolic repatriation in some form—be it creative, artistic, linguistic, in dream content, or in actual return visits or return migration. Such expression may be as much a requisite for effective psychological integration for migrant individuals and their families as is effectively learning the new culture and coping with its demands (Maduro and Martinez 1974; Paris 1978: Kunz 1981). Recent epidemiological data have confirmed results of clinical investigations on the effects of acculturation on mental health. Significant associations were found for alcohol and drug abuse and dependence, phobia, and antisocial personality with high levels of acculturation of Mexican-Americans, while culturally rooted and immigrant Mexicans exhibited much lower prevalence rates (Vega et al. 1984; Warheit et al. 1985; Burnam et al. 1987).

In the next chapter, the specific context of immigration is presented for the Guatemalan families described in this study. The context provides a map for understanding how and why they came to be where they are today. What are the psychological demands on these families of their past?

THE QUETZAL IN FLIGHT

GUATEMALAN EXODUS

The present-day structural conditions that set the stage for Guatemalan emigration are principally four in number: (1) demographic growth patterns, (2) land use policy, (3) U.S. ambivalence toward investment and military involvement, and (4) glaring social and cultural schisms and inequities among the Guatemalan people themselves maintained by a police state.

Among the Central American countries, Guatemala has the largest population, about 9 million (Menchú 1990). It is currently undergoing "phase two" of the demographic transition—from a situation in which both birth and death rates are high and thus balanced, to a situation in which birth and death rates will be balanced at lower rates. In the transition phase, particularly in nonindustrial countries and countries where there is competitive allocation of land (where large landowners are free to dispossess numerous small landowners), the death rate falls (except for infant mortality, which remains high) but the fertility rate stays high and population soars. In such situations it is to the benefit of the poor peasant family to have a large family; thus, the complete transition (the lowering of the fertility rate) does not take place. This has been occurring in Guatemala, especially in the rural areas, and there has been a consequent population explosion as well as a severe and growing problem of childhood malnutrition (as high as 82 percent among children under the age of five) (Early 1982).

Scarcity and maldistribution of land is on the increase as well. The problem is somewhat like that existing in El Salvador, although El Salvador's extreme population density pushed its crisis to peak earlier. In El Salvador, inequitable land tenure and consequent migration across the border into Honduras were direct causes of the so-called Soccer War of 1968 with Honduras and were an antecedent to the recent civil strife

(Durham 1977; Ehrlich et al. 1979). Similarly, Indian peasants in Guatemala once worked communal land plots and fed their own communities. In the late nineteenth century, Guatemalan president Barrios ("the reformer") decided to create an export economy based primarily on coffee *fincas*. To accomplish this, communal land systems were outlawed and Indians were forced to become seasonal laborers working on foreign-owned plantations (Warren 1978). The main effect of this change in the agricultural economy has been the deterioration of subsistence farming, which forms the basis of the peasant economy. According to the 1964 census, 87.4 percent of the farms were too small to support a family. More than three-fourths of the population was landless or land-poor (Davis 1983). Now, approximately two-thirds of the arable land is owned by 2.2 percent of the land owners (Episcopado Guatemalteco 1988).

Foreign-owned plantations (with owners primarily in the United States) have increasingly suffered social and economic problems through boom and bust cycles. In the early 1970s plantation owners started evicting squatters. In the late 1970s there was a notable increase in labor unrest, strikes, and sabotage. Moreover, the increasingly repressive tactics used at the time by Guatemalan military and paramilitary forces decreased U.S. readiness to finance huge military aid packages, as had been done in the 1960s. During the Reagan and Bush administrations, the same kind of ambivalent interventionist moves that characterized the U.S. involvement in Vietnam have been played out all over Central America, including Guatemala, with a number of the same figures as in the Vietnam era in government and military positions (White 1984). Also, a good deal of U.S. financial support for the current militarily-controlled regime in Guatemala takes place in the name of humanitarian aid used to pay off foreign debt, thus freeing the budget for military means. Private religious organizations and U.S. aid to other countries, particularly Israel, provide additional conduits for perpetuation of the Guatemalan military. The final factor of significance in shaping structural conditions in Guatemala is its deep social and cultural schism. In other Central American countries, *mestizaje* (racial mixture and ethnic assimilation) and proletarianization were imposed at an earlier date. In contrast, Guatemalan social and cultural contradictions have been longstanding and unresolved (Brintnall 1979a; 1979b). Schisms and inequities are perhaps the greatest between Indians and *Ladinos* (primarily Indian-Spanish *mestizos* who are culturally Hispanicized) based on a caste system that is four centuries old. But divisions also exist between Catholics and Protestant evangelicals (Burnett 1986), the political right and left, men and women, urban and rural peoples, and highland and lowland regions. Caste distinctions and the integrity of Indian identity are now attenuated in the process of forced acculturation and migration. Indians can no longer close their corporate boundaries, as the military infiltrates everywhere and land and cash are scarce. They are forced into an accommodation with the Ladinoization process (Warren 1978; Early 1982). Manz has studied the social landscape of present-day Guatemalan internal refugees:

The role of the military and paramilitary organizations in even the most isolated communities has engendered divisiveness, fear, and mistrust. Not since the Spanish conquest have the highlands seen such a cultural breakdown. Moreover, although Indians were aware of their powerlessness vis-à-vis economic and political elites and the army, fear for their lives did not dominate their activities and consciousness. (1988, p. 12)

Many Indian and Ladino peasants cope by joining seasonal migration streams. The Mexico-Guatemala border runs right through Indian communities in a jungle region where migrant farm workers have traditionally worked the coffee harvest. *Comerciantes* (small businessmen or vendors), sharecroppers, and wage laborers move from town to town, the Indians (especially the men) affecting Ladino clothing and speaking Spanish. Over 35 percent of the internal migration in Guatemala is to Guatemala City, the one large city in the country where over 35 percent of the population lives. This influx is all quite recent, and most migrants have joined the ranks of the lower-class urban poor in shantytowns at the outskirts of town. The industrial sector is not expanding, so there is minimal working-class consciousness. Rather, the new labor force takes on service and commercial ventures. Caste distinctions become less salient, and the lives of these urbanites are dominated by multiple dependencies and loyalties, obligations to competing Catholic and evangelizing Protestant churches, and patron and family networks. Conservative political forces have also helped to stifle the potential political influence of so many dissatisfied and frustrated shantytown dwellers. Most observers have shown these poor families to be fearful and distrustful of any form of organization (Roberts 1973; Early 1982; Perera 1986; Manz 1988).

What are the bases for these current population, social, and cultural pressures and dynamics; the land use policy; and U.S. involvement in the Guatemalan landscape? In tracing their origins, it is instructive to review relevant aspects of Guatemalan and Mesoamerican history.

Guatemala, like other Central American countries, has been the object of foreign intervention and control throughout its history. Foreign domination of the native population did not begin with the Spanish crown. Central America as a whole suffered incursions by other indigenous kingdoms (especially Aztec and Toltec) centuries prior to the Spanish invasion. The native population also felt the effects of forays from South America, although these were less militaristic and, therefore, less consequential. In general, though, inhabitants of Central America had dealt with direct imposition of foreign control (or at least its threat) long before Spaniards set foot on the land. There is a long and rich history of indigenous resistance and revolt to such oppression which continues up to the present day. As historical background, this information puts the contemporary era of U.S. involvement in the region into perspective.

The Spanish conquest was especially brutal in Guatemala, and it took a good deal longer to accomplish than in other parts of Mesoamerica. Pedro de Alvarado and his forces were conquering territory somewhat removed from Spain's primary goals in central Mexico. Thus, the military band was unencumbered by legal and religious scruples in their dealings with the indigenous communities and leaders they encountered. During this period in particular, there were widespread hostilities and resistance on the part of numerous decentralized and isolated Indian kingdoms and communities. Rebellions and uprisings slackened during periods of dramatic population decline, but they increased when the population revived and began to grow again in the nineteenth century (Helms 1975).

Other European adventurers began to rival Spain in their interest in Guatemala and Central America throughout the centuries before independence. Due to the isolation of vast regions of Central America and Spain's internal preoccupations, intense competition developed among British, Dutch, and French smugglers and pirates. The Caribbean Islands were generally used as staging arenas for colonial and pirateering exploits on the Atlantic mainland. Interest in coffee and banana plantations, forestry, and mining developed as additional motivating factors (Palacio 1982).

In the century following the conquest, native population declined drastically by about 50 to 95 percent, depending on the area. Coastal regions and communities that had more contact with malaria, Spaniards, and other foreigners suffered the most extensive depopulation. This took place through epidemics, war, flight, enslavement, and racial mixture with Spaniards and Black slaves. Highland Indian communities located in less temperate climates and those existing in greater numbers proportionate to conquerors and colonizers could better resist and survive the Spanish intrusion. They did so by means of closed corporate communities, which developed to more exclusivity in the nineteenth century (MacLeod 1973).

Overall, the impact of Spanish domination was such that Indian identity was essentially re-formed as an adaptive response. The outside pressures were those of colonial Catholicism, community resettlement, and the use of Indians as the primary labor force in a variety of labor systems (slavery, *encomienda, repartamiento*, debt peonage, sharecropping, plantation, and "free" labor). The crown stopped short of an extermination and/or enclave policy (as was practiced by U.S. pioneer settlers vis-à-vis Native Americans). Instead, the Spanish colonial empire saw agriculture as its primary interest and took advantage of indigenous social and economic organizations when it could exploit them. Initially, the *encomienda* system involved Spanish administration of Indian communities that continued to own their own land, supplying tribute through hierarchical channels to Spain. Thus, Spanish racial and religious ideology (Indians were souls to be saved) and economic need established a centralized Spanish superstructure over an already effective farming and marketing system (Wolf 1956; Helms 1975).

The survival and revitalization of the indigenous people of Guatemala as distinctive groups, as well as the maintenance of twenty-two languages and associated traditions constitute a stunning accomplishment for the descendants of the once-advanced Mayan civilization. Yet the struggle for survival and ethnic integrity among the indigenous people continues. Indians still face excruciating poverty, oppression, and massacres; they occupy a structural position in the primarily agricultural peasant caste society that has remained basically unchanged since the conquest.

In 1821, Central America declared independence from Spain. *Criollos* (Spanish, but Guatemalan born) led the colonial movement. True independence, however, was ephemeral. The Central American economy was based on the needs of foreign markets; no unifying national character was allowed to develop among the population. Instead, it was divided among the warring *caudillos* (chiefs) and was separated from Indian communities. The growing *criollo* and *Ladino* (children of unions between Indians and Spaniards) population had no clear economic or power base in the society. Together, as "bastard children," they were unable to find social positions through their parents or their livelihood in the cities or Indian communities. They became a mobile workforce instead—vagabonds and tradesmen—and they joined the armies of the *caudillos*. Thus, via independence, they simultaneously created a power vacuum and filled it. Mounting a succession of military governments, Central America became divided into more easily controlled geographical units, what are now the Central American nations that share a similar colonial history and political economy. These are Guatemala, El Salvador, Honduras, Nicaragua, and Costa Rica (Smith and Boyer 1987).

As one of these nations, Guatemala is now undergoing a protracted revolution. It is similar to the one just waged in El Salvador and the one being somewhat reversed in Nicaragua, and yet it is different in other ways. Like other Central American revolutions, Guatemala's internal upheaval is associated with foreign intervention, an export economy (a boom from 1954 to 1976), population growth, and a growing gulf between the small numbers of the powerful elite and large numbers of landless peasants.

In recent times a series of events has brought Guatemala to its current high level of militarization and terror:

1. In the early 1960s, the United States trained forces in Guatemala for the abortive Bay of Pigs invasion of Cuba. The Guatemalan military became polarized in its reaction to the U.S. initiative. A small band of mostly younger dissident military men led guerrilla forces in rebel maneuvers in eastern Guatemala.

2. At the same time as military polarization was taking place, the Catholic Church began to fear a shift in the established religious order (due to stimulation by ideas from evangelism, liberation theology, Marxism, and assimilationism). In response, the Catholic Church organized a revitalization of the rural and Indian sectors.

3. The Catholic Action projects (rural cooperatives, agricultural development, spontaneous colonization) ran headlong into conflict with the expansionist interests of military generals and mining and petroleum concerns represented by the Land Institute. Backed by the military, the Land Institute intervened to keep the contested lands vacant for cattle grazing, mining, and drilling. With the establishment of the Central American Common Market, market expansion took place and many new jobs were created in the lowland coastal regions. But poor and Indian migrant workers were generally paid extremely low wages, were often cheated when they were paid, and were made sick by exposure to high levels of herbicides and pesticides. Many of the workers refused to return to the backbreaking work; they left in droves for work in small business and construction and as artisans. Plantation owners hired Salvadorans when labor shortages began to occur, but the working class–conscious Salvadorans immediately initiated organized work stoppages and strikes.

4. In the late 1960s, the United States spent over $17 million in direct military aid to suppress guerrilla activity (about 300 men) in eastern Guatemala. This was the beginning of the death squads and the stepped-up violence—massacres and Vietnam-style counterinsurgency—

both in the cities and in the countryside (Adams 1970; Warren 1978; Davis 1983). Suffering the loss of their land and massive military repression, many Indians and *Ladinos* joined the guerrilla resistance, which was made up of four organizations—*Ejército Guerrillero de los Pobres* (EGP), *Organización Revolucionaria del Pueblo en Armas* (ORPA), *Fuerzas Armadas Rebeldes* (FAR), and *Partido Guatemalteco del Trabajo* (PGT).

5. The final contributing event was the 1976 earthquake, which left 22,000 dead, 77,000 injured, and over a million homeless. In the rural highlands, close to 90 percent of all homes were destroyed or damaged. The result of this disaster was twofold: (1) International and private religious and other aid groups provided relief, and this increased contact with foreigners; and (2) Popular and local groups got a taste of what they could accomplish in rebuilding their homes and livelihoods through their own independent action. Many people involved as independent operators or as recipients of aid noted that large funds for relief ended up lining the pockets of government functionaries and that cooperative local efforts toward rebuilding safer homes threatened the status quo. Death threats and staff disappearances halted much of the organized relief efforts of some private aid groups (Fried et al. 1983; Eckholm 1984).

Guatemala's experience differs from other Central American countries in some other important ways. First, it is unique among Central American countries in its striking social contrasts. Because it served as an intellectual, governing, and religious colonial center for Central America, it has always attracted elites, including a substantial number of European immigrants. At the same time, its Indian and peasant populations are the largest and poorest in Central America; Guatemala is second only to Haiti in Latin American poverty statistics (Davis 1983). Second, Guatemala's proximity to the United States has led to U.S. readiness to invest in the region—$226 million worth (Ferris 1987)—due to its labor supply and potential for oil and other minerals. Third, Guatemala has already had experience with sweeping electoral reformation.

In the 1940s, because of a growing economy, a strong middle class was forming and articulating the need for U.S.-style, New Deal–type democratic reforms. An electoral victory in 1944 by Arévalo began a process of social experimentation, or what Adams calls "secondary development" as opposed to "primary" or technological development (Adams 1967, p. 3). This era of social invention was institutionalized through democratic means and lasted until 1954, when U.S. opposition to what was felt to be communist influence in the government led to a

(U.S.-sponsored) coup, the dismantling of the social experiments, and the return of the police state. As a result, Guatemalans have tasted the beginnings of land reform, effective unionization, development of constitutional rights, and educational reform. Their loss has made the contradictions in the social landscape more poignant. These contradictions have continued throughout the 1980s in the war between guerrilla fighters and the military, with Indian peasants most often caught up as victims of army sweeps and massacres in the villages. Consequently, a large Indian refugee population can be found living internally (estimated at 300,000 in Guatemala City alone), in camps in Campeche and Quintana Roo departments of Mexico, and along the Mexican border with Guatemala (Fuentes 1981; Kinzer and Schlesinger 1981; Immerman 1982; Fried et al. 1983; *San Francisco Examiner* 1982; Gutierrez 1984; Smith 1984; Ferris 1987). Many villages have been repopulated as military strategic hamlets with the army in total control. The civilian populace is obliged to form militias to enforce army control. Since there is little salaried work in the model villages, these sites are becoming repositories for widows and orphans, while the more adventurous have taken to the road looking for work or are in hiding in the mountains (Smith 1984; Manz 1988).

It is clear that the struggle raging now in Guatemala is related to the aborted peaceful attempt at reconciliation in the 1940s and 1950s. It may be argued that Mexico, too, has not been able to find a solution to its own ongoing economic crisis, its unraveling social and political infrastructure, its population growth, and its consequent high rate of out-migration to the United States.[1] However, in contrast to Guatemala, Mexico has been able to conclude its successful revolution in the early decades of this century. Through this experience, the Mexican nation has forged a national art and intelligentsia centered on *mestizaje* and Indianism as well as land reform and the *ejido* movement. Guatemala lacks this sense of national identity and purpose because its own social development has been stifled by the return of the police state.

I see the significance of aborted national ideology and identity as being crucial for Guatemalan families, particularly those who are finding it necessary to escape an economic nightmare of inflation, unemployment, and physical vulnerability to violence. Historically, social and ethnic identity has had its effects on the Guatemalan family structure in that a caste society provides few options for people in the middle—those who are *mestizos*, middle class, who belong neither in a social niche in a village economy nor in a protected network of the elite and powerful.

Guatemalan historian Severo Martinez Palaez puts it dramatically:

Let us understand, then, that the initial interbreeding was an act realized in the context of and as a consequence of the societal inferiority and disadvantage of a woman from the dominated class facing a man from the dominant class. It was the result of a biological union based on profound human disunion and inequality; of fornication as an act of veiled domination, or, in many cases, simple and open outrage. The children of these unions, the original half-breeds were what they were—workers without patrimony, tossed out in search of middle-level occupations or completely unskilled ones—as a consequence of their parents belonging to two antagonistic classes; and neither could give them a place without bringing harm to their class or themselves. . . .

The secondary interbreeding . . . was a proliferating of individuals in search of middle-level and inferior vacant positions and occupations. Individuals without inherited property, or authority, or servants, had to make themselves useful in order to be remunerated and in order to survive. . . . The need for free workers acted as a mold into which the human stream of half-breeds was poured. (1976, pp. 355-360)

SIX FAMILIES IN FLIGHT

Conflicto, Aventura, y Muerte—Ido de Sentido: The Menchú-Franzi Family

Origins

I met the Menchú-Franzi family following a telephone call I received from their nineteen-year-old son, Miguel. He was a student at an English language school in San Francisco's heavily Latino district, the Mission. The director of the school suggested to him that he might want to participate in my study.

The Menchú-Franzi household is a blended family or stepfamily consisting of Olga and Antonio Franzi, the husband and wife, and the young adult children of both of them. At various times during the period in which I interviewed this family, there were from two to five of these children and one grandchild living in the household with their parents.

Olga came to the United States to stay ten years ago. Her adult children were all born and raised in Guatemala and are more recent immigrants to the United States than she is. Those living in the Menchú-Franzi household are Alma, age 25; Graciela, age 22; and Miguel, age 19. Graciela also has a two-year-old daughter, Lidia. For case study purposes, Miguel is the identified Guatemalan adolescent immigrant in this family.

Antonio is an Argentine immigrant; he has lived in the United States for forty-seven years. His adult children were born in the United States although their mother, like Olga, was a Guatemalan immigrant. Victor, age 22, lives in the household, and for a time during my interviewing, so did América, age 20.

Olga, at age 50, is a plucky, expressive, and attractive woman who has been married three times and has had seven children. She was born in a small village in the Petén, or easternmost jungle region of Guatemala. Her mother was from a remote but large town in the central highlands, and her father was Mexican. From the age of six to sixteen, she was *internada* (sent to school) in her mother's birthplace, Cobán. When Olga became sixteen, her father left her mother and returned to Mexico.

At first, after her father left, Olga went to Guatemala City and stayed with her *madrina* (godmother), learning dressmaking. But a year later she decided to return to the Petén, where she married and started a family. Mr. Menchú, Olga's first husband, was the father of six of her children (Julián, Eduardo, Alma, Tomás, Graciela, and Miguel). He was a contractor working in gum and wood. After a few years of marriage, he began to mistreat her.

Olga tired of being beaten by her husband. When she found that he had another woman, she decided to move her entire family to Guatemala City in the care of one of her brothers who was living there. She worked there to raise her children on the $100 per month that her husband sent her plus her own earnings as a seamstress and from occasional factory work. Her mother also lived with her, helping with the children. Sewing was lonely and factory work was oppressive, but Olga says that she knew then that she would never return to her life in the Petén even if she had to sweep or wash clothes for a living.

Antonio Franzi, at age 77, is Olga's third husband. He is a well-traveled, four-times-married, retired adventurer. He was born in Italy in 1906 and migrated to Argentina at the age of ten with friends of his father, leaving his family behind in Italy. In Argentina he lived with his father's brother's family and attended school briefly, but he mostly worked alongside his uncle and cousins building roads, doing farm work, waiting on tables in restaurants, and serving as a nursing assistant in a hospital. He laughs when he says that he loved to work and to be on the move: "*somos brutos*" ("we are rough brutes"). When Antonio was sixteen, his mother sent his father over from Italy to bring him home, but he wouldn't return. Instead, he stayed, married, had two sons, and shortly thereafter joined the Argentine navy. Six years at sea traveling around the world and a young woman he met made him curious about the United States. He emigrated here in 1936, worked in San Francisco as a cook, and finally settled in Fresno as an agricultural foreman overseeing Mexican farmworkers.

In Fresno, Antonio married a Mexican woman with whom he lived for twenty-four years although they had no children together. During this time he petitioned for his grown son Jorge to come to the United States from Argentina along with Jorge's wife and children. (His other Argentine son had died as a child.) Antonio set Jorge up in Sacramento, California. Antonio divorced his second wife when he was fifty-five. He was vague about the reasons, intimating that she was an alcoholic.

Shortly after this divorce, Antonio met and married a Guatemalan immigrant with whom he had his two U.S.-born children, Victor and América. This marriage lasted for ten years, and Antonio was again divorced for reasons that he was reticent to divulge.

In 1975, Antonio was introduced to Olga as a woman who needed help in establishing her residency in the United States. Olga was impressed with the advice "Don Antonio" was able to give her, and Antonio was impressed with Olga. They were married in 1976.

The Decision to Move

Olga's emigration to the United States and to the San Francisco Bay Area is a tale with many tragic twists and turns. Olga describes herself as a woman who has always fought to overcome obstacles and injustice, and to persevere.

Olga first began thinking about coming to the United States on the advice of a friend in Guatemala City who told her about how much money it was possible to make in the United States. As her friend had been living in the San Francisco Bay Area, she helped Olga obtain a tourist visa; Olga came for the first time in 1969 and stayed for ten months. During this time she worked as a live-in babysitter, leaving her own children (then ranging in ages from six to sixteen) in the care of her mother in Guatemala City.

Olga returned to Guatemala briefly to visit her family and then came back to the United States in 1971 for ten more months of work. During this second interval in the United States, she found work through newspaper ads and through friends. She also found a man, a *pocho* (half Mexican, half American), with whom she fell in love, got married, and became pregnant. Her seventh child was a boy, Ricardo, whom she left in the care of her husband when she returned to Guatemala for her eldest son Julián's graduation from high school. She had planned to apply for her U.S. residency through her new husband, but when she called him from Guatemala, he said that he no longer wanted her and for her to stay in Guatemala.

It took Olga a year to accumulate enough money to get back to the United States. This time she had a different motive, to be reunited with her young son. Friends advised her to seek out Don Antonio, who knew about these kinds of problems. He was well known as having lots of experience with legal matters. He helped her to get a lawyer, to take back her toddler son (with police backup), and, again, make application for residency through her U.S.-born offspring. (At that time, in 1975, it was still possible to apply on this basis.) Olga and Antonio were married the following year.

Around this time, Eduardo, Olga's second oldest son, entered the United States. He was nineteen, and, according to his brother Miguel, he came because he had a problem "in the streets. He had been in a gang. There had been trouble, a fight, and Eduardo had shot—not killed—someone in self-defense." So he had to leave the country immediately. His uncle, Olga's youngest brother (with whom the family was living), helped him get the cash and connections to leave the country without delay. Eduardo first went to Villahermosa, Mexico, to stay with another uncle, and finally he came to the San Francisco Bay Area with the help of his uncle in Villahermosa. When he came to the Bay Area, he quickly decided to stay even though he had word from home that all was forgiven and that he would not be charged in the shooting. Instead, he settled in the Mission District, married a Salvadoran woman, and now has two babies.

In 1979, Olga brought her young son, Ricardo, to Guatemala to meet the rest of the family. While they were visiting, Ricardo, then six, was killed in an accident. He was crushed by a truck while he was playing in front of the house. Olga is extremely bitter about this accident, saying that the driver got away on a hit and run charge and that many neighbors who witnessed the event denied they saw anything because they didn't want to "get involved." This event assured her that she did not want to live in Guatemala again.

In February 1981, Julián, Olga's oldest son (age 27), who by then was a well-known figure at the University of San Carlos, was suddenly machine-gunned to death by thugs who entered the university. Eight other university students and faculty were also gunned down, and ten were injured in the political assassination. This had a profound effect on Miguel, who at age 17 was Olga's youngest son (except for Ricardo, who had been killed two years before); Miguel was devastated. He had been studying drafting, but when his brother was murdered he became upset—*ido de sentido*—and he couldn't concentrate any more. He says he was depressed and stayed in his room all the time. Once when he went outside he thought he saw a car following him; he ran and got away, but he was frightened. No one was ever charged in the murders and shootings of his brother and the others at the university; it seemed to be a death squad type of activity. Later that year Miguel went to Villahermosa to visit his uncle, as Eduardo had done five years previously. From there, his mother convinced him to come to the United States. She had already petitioned for his residency, and by this time it had been approved. She sent him the airfare and he was able to fly to San Francisco easily as a permanent resident under his mother's petition.

In the Menchú-Franzi family, the prime mover and center in the family with regard to the decision to come to the United States is Olga, the mother. It was she who originally chose to come here on her own, leaving her children in the care of her family in Guatemala. And it was she who eventually decided to bring them up when the deteriorating atmosphere in her home country resulted in the tragic deaths of her sons. Although Eduardo and, subsequently, Graciela independently found their own way to the United States, all four of her children are living near her now, which indicates the leadership and power she exerts in the family.

The Journey and Settling In

Olga's children are the most recent immigrants in the Menchú-Franzi family. With the exception of Eduardo, who came in 1975, all have been in the United States for less than three years. Therefore, in interviewing this family, I focused on their experiences in coming to the United States and particularly on the experience of the adolescent son, Miguel.

Miguel saw the journey to the United States as a momentous one for him, a change of life. Although he had many reasons of his own for coming to the United States, his mother's petition had the most immediate impact. Some of the other factors that influenced his attitude about coming were the following: He had many acquaintances (about twenty, he says) who had come to the United States, and his best friend from Guatemala was living in Ohio. He also had a girlfriend who was pressuring him to marry her; he wanted to escape this dilemma since he felt that he was not ready for marriage. Finally, Miguel was even more convinced of the rightness of his decision when, only a few weeks after he left Guatemala, his last brother living at home, Tomás (then 23) was also gunned down in an ambush. Tomás was working for his uncle installing a heater in a customer's home, doing the same kind of work that Miguel had been doing before he left Guatemala. The killer took $250 that Tomás had been paid as well as his watch. Miguel does not know why this happened or who was responsible. He and his family do see it as another political killing, though, which suggests that there may be more to this story than they either know or wish to tell.

Naturally, the news of this new loss was traumatic for Miguel. His enthusiasm for the struggle to "make it" in the new environment was dampened. As before with the death of his eldest brother, he took to his room. He did not leave his mother's apartment for over a month. When he attempted to make tentative moves outside to look for work and friendship, he felt very embarrassed over not knowing any English. "People laughed at me." When he was able to communicate, he did not like the cold and impersonal style of social relations that he found to be the rule, and he did not like the lack of real friendship.

In terms of work and education, back in Guatemala Miguel had left off studying drafting after the death of his first brother. In addition to working for his uncle in Guatemala City installing heaters, he had also apprenticed with another uncle during a visit to Mexico and had begun to learn offset printing. So far, he had only learned to print in black and white. He attempted to use his beginning training to find some work in the San Francisco area, but he was told that it was impossible for him to start without connections, without knowing English, and without more training in color printing. Community college classes in offset printing were already filled.

Miguel became discouraged. Too old for high school, he enrolled in an adult school English class in the Mission District. Because it was too far to commute from his mother and stepfather's apartment in South San Francisco, he moved in with his brother Eduardo. He got a job at a car wash. Thus began a period in which he tried to adapt all at once to his new life in the United States. There were several wrong turns on this path. Miguel became frustrated with the car wash job. All of the other workers were friends of the manager, and they spent their time fooling around, having fun, while they pressured him to work harder doing their work.

Feeling isolated and alone, Miguel attempted to make friends with other young men who could teach him English. He met one Latino youth "on the street," who recruited Miguel into a *pandilla* (gang) of *cholos*. Miguel's loneliness and desire to be part of a group of friends led him to go along with whatever they were doing. There were eight other gang members; all of them had lived in the United States for at least five years. They all spoke English and taught Miguel black street talk, such as "What's happening?" Five of them were Salvadoran; two were Nicaraguan; one was Guatemalan. They ranged in age from 17 to 20. Most of them no longer lived with their families; a few of them were enrolled at Mission High School (but they did not actually attend classes). Their activities consisted mainly of "hanging out" in the park, smoking marijuana, snorting cocaine, and taking turns robbing liquor stores. When it looked like it was going to be Miguel's turn to rob a store he decided to leave this group. Also at this time he developed a problem with his nasal cartilage that affected his breathing, and he had an operation to correct this. (His cocaine use at this time might have exacerbated or even caused the problem.) At any rate, Miguel decided on his own to leave the gang life behind him.

During the time I was interviewing the family, Miguel had moved back home with his mother and stepfather. He had a job in a gas station and was studying English. He met a new girlfriend in one of his classes and began spending all of his free time with her. In fact, although he was living with his mother and stepfather, he was not actually spending much time with them. He studied English, took classes toward the G.E.D. test (high school equivalency exam), worked, and spent the balance of his free time with his girlfriend. This included staying overnight at her house on weekends.

Fourteen months after Miguel entered the United States, his twenty-five-year-old sister Alma came, and four months later the last of the Menchú children, Graciela (age 23), arrived. Alma had to wait in Guatemala for eight months for her petition for permanent residence to be approved. Graciela decided to come on her own via Mexico and a visit with her father. She and her infant daughter somehow ended up in Tijuana for a while until she was finally able to cross the border. There are now three Menchú children and one grandchild crowding the small south city apartment.

The arrival of the first Guatemalan daughter, Alma, precipitated an immediate clash with América, Antonio's twenty-year-old daughter. Sharing a bedroom, Alma discovered to her shock that América was using cocaine. She reported this to América's father, Antonio, who did nothing. América, however, was angry at the cheek of the unwanted interloper into her life, and tore apart all of Alma's belongings, ripped up her clothes, and left a pile on the floor of the bedroom. Meanwhile, Alma had begun a correspondence with a Guatemalan man who was living in Los Angeles. She had never met him but had found his name and address in a magazine personals column. Alma, distraught at how things had been going while living as a new arrival in the stepfamily and with no prospects of work, accepted his marriage proposal over her mother's objection, and went to Los Angeles. América also decided to leave; her father arranged for her to go to live with her maternal aunt in Miami.

After three months, Alma returned to her mother's home. Her brief marriage had been a nightmare. Her husband had insisted that she stay home all day long in a tiny apartment. He didn't want her to work, take classes, or have any friends. When she objected, he beat her. This went on until she had an attack of hysteria and was hospitalized on a psychiatric ward for a few days. After this, she wanted no part of him. Back home, she is now anxiously anticipating looking for work as a babysitter. She has great ambitions of being an elementary schoolteacher. But her sense of shame and her fears are making it difficult for her to even take a step toward conversational English classes. Although Alma studied English for years in Guatemala, she was afraid to say a word to me in English because of her *vergüenza* (shame).

In addition to the clash between Alma and América, the family is somewhat divided on the subject of Victor, Antonio's son. Although Antonio is obviously worried about América who flits back into the Bay Area from Miami only to travel to Las Vegas, to Reno, to Sausalito, and to New York with a "rich girlfriend" (Drugs? they wonder. Prostitution?) whom they have never met, Victor is another story. Victor has graduated from community college and now has a good job with the telephone company. Moreover, Victor has applied to be a California highway patrolman. They are waiting for the results of his test. But Olga, Antonio's wife, and Alma and Graciela, her daughters, are not at all impressed with Victor. They all feel he is arrogant, ill-mannered, and disrespectful. Moreover, he has a black girlfriend of whom Olga and Antonio do not approve. Miguel has reserved judgment on Victor since he is the only other young male in the household.

As for Miguel, Olga and Antonio worry about him. They feel he is being taken advantage of by his girlfriend and her aunt. Olga is afraid that the girl will become pregnant. She also worries because he chauffeurs the young woman and her aunt all over town in their car and he really doesn't know his way around. He has had one car accident in which his driver's license was suspended because he hit a parked car and left the scene of the accident, being fearful of dealing with the police. He also has to pay $3,000 in damages out of his earnings now, so that cuts back on the family income. Antonio has advised Miguel to go into the U.S. Navy. For this reason, Miguel is attempting to take and pass the G.E.D. test as a requisite to joining the navy. He thinks he should be able to get a good education through the navy. He and his family agree that it would add discipline and structure to his life, that he has been too affected here by all of the *libertad,* or license.

All in all, everyone is looking for a way out of this uncomfortably blended family. There is talk about Miguel, Alma, and Graciela (with

Lidia) getting an apartment together when all are working and bringing in good salaries. Miguel might go into the navy. He also might move in with an older woman as a boarder in San Francisco. América is already out of the home but is conducting (perhaps) some "dirty business," according to her father, in which he feels helpless to intervene. Victor might join the highway patrol and then move out of the home. Mr. and Mrs. Franzi do not like their apartment or their neighborhood. They are fed up with the robberies and bad character of the street they live on. Even the rent is going up. Antonio wants to find senior citizen housing, which would force the issue with the adult children. Olga wants to live in San Francisco—not in the Mission District where there is too much trouble, but in some more peaceful neighborhood.

The Adolescent and the Family Culture

There are three main themes in the family culture of the Menchú-Franzis: conflict (*conflicto*), adventure (*aventura*), and death (*muerte*). All of these apply to the family's view of youth. The family is in a loyalty bind between the children of Olga and the children of Antonio. What is more significant is that the conflict indicates a clash of values between the U.S.-born children and those who were born in Guatemala and who are recent immigrants.

For example, an incident involving Victor (U.S.-born) occurred toward the end of my interviews with the family. Tension started to build in the home when Mrs. Franzi lost her full-time job as a hotel maid. She was cut back to only two days a week. At the same time, Alma was not working, Graciela was doing only a little babysitting, and Miguel was spending all of his time completing examinations for his G.E.D. certificate. Financially, things were very tight for the whole family. Victor was the only one living in the household who had a steady job. He generally did not contribute much to the family expenses, according to Olga but instead saved his earnings in a bank account for himself. Family pressure began to build for him to contribute something to the household, but Victor resisted. The pressure erupted one day when Victor became angry at dinnertime; he didn't like what Olga had cooked and he threw it across the room. There was a lot of yelling, some slapping, and, according to Mrs. Franzi, Victor threatened to kill members of her family, and then locked himself in the bathroom. Neighbors heard the yelling and called the police. The police dealt with it as a family quarrel, and nothing was done. Antonio tried to act as peacemaker, but he generally took Victor's side in the argument.

These value conflicts show up on the Moos Family Environment Scale

(Appendix 2 describes the family evaluation testing that was conducted) in that the two highest scores for the family as a whole are moral-religious orientation and conflict orientation (see Figure 1). Family members have strong beliefs and consistent clashes over what they feel is moral and correct. The lowest score on the Moos is in cohesion. Notably, Antonio, the stepfather who is the family member most "in the middle," scores the lowest in cohesion. (Family incongruence or disagreement is scored at 18, which is somewhat higher than average.) These low scores in cohesion and high scores in family incongruence do not mean that family support and bonding are unimportant to the Menchú-Franzi family. On the contrary, results of the Family Adaptability and Cohesion Scale (FACES) indicate that most family members would like the family to be closer than they now are (see Figure 2). (The U.S.-born children and Graciela did not participate in the testing.) Mr. and Mrs. Franzi would like them to move from disengagement to "separated engagement." Miguel yearns for extremely close or "enmeshed engagement."

Adventure is another common theme for this family. All family members are somewhat rebellious, and they desire "chaotic adaptability" in the family setting as opposed to what they see as its present rigidity (see Figure 2). All members love to travel; they see it as exciting, uplifting, and even as a necessary part of life. Antonio regards his life as that of a rogue adventurer, although now he is really much more a stable homebody. At age 77 and with a heart condition, he still dreams of traveling back to Italy with Olga. Olga told me of a recurring dream she has in which she is back home in the village where she was born, walking up a mountain looking for Antonio. She says people tell her, "If you go too far, you'll get lost." She wanders and wanders and does become lost. She has a similar dream in which she is looking for her sons who are in danger. Perhaps she does feel she has gone too far away from what is familiar and that she has lost herself. She, too, may be *ido de sentido*.

The third theme for this family is that of death and loss. This family has suffered four deaths in four years, mostly of young men. In 1979, Ricardo, Olga's seventh child, was run over by a truck at the age of six. In 1981, Julián, Olga's firstborn, an up-and-coming leader in the law and in the arts, was assassinated in a mass killing. That same year, Antonio lost his eldest son to a heart attack at the age of 50. Finally, in 1982, Olga's third son was murdered in an ambush. All of these deaths have muted this family's natural exuberance and adventurous spirit. Although the family attends Catholic church services on Sundays, they engage in no other family-oriented social activities. Both Olga and Antonio used

FIGURE 1 - The Menchú-Franzi Family

Family Environment Scale

(FES)

Family Incongruence Score = 18

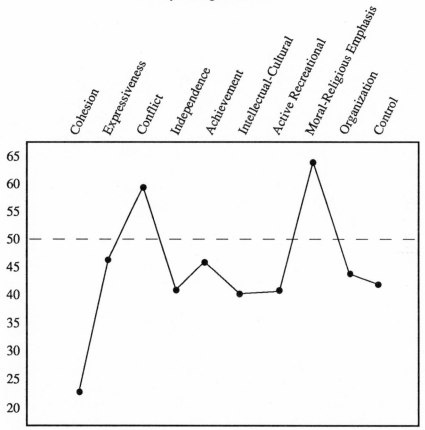

FIGURE 2 - The Menchú-Franzi Family

Family Adaptability and Cohesion Scale
(FACES)

Family Discrepancy Score = 23.2

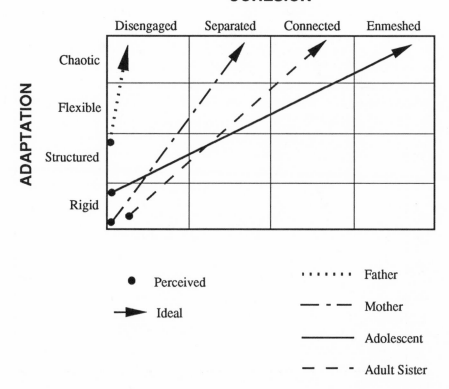

COHESION

to belong to the Club Guatemalteco and the Club Argentino, and they used to like to go out dancing. In the last five years, however, for the parents there have been no social activities, no friends outside the family. They have been in mourning, and there has been a strong feeling of depression and anger in the home. The energy level for perseverance and struggle is also somewhat dimmer. Mrs. Franzi had no job the last time I saw her. She was not about to go stand in line at the hotel workers' union just to be told nothing was available. She was tired. She had not had a vacation in two years, and so, it appears, she was taking one. Alma, Graciela, and Miguel still seem to be somewhat *ido de sentido*. Although they are trying their best to help out, life is still quite difficult for all of the family.

Éxito y Sacrificio: The Walter Family

Origins

A Cuban expatriate who had served as a community worker, restauranteur, teacher, and lay Catholic leader referred me to this family. She had heard through her grapevine of their arrival, and she had helped them in obtaining some furniture.

The Walter family is a household of seven members. There were eight members when I began interviewing them, but soon thereafter the paternal grandfather, who had been living with the family only temporarily, moved out. The other seven members are the parents, Mr. and Mrs. Walter; their three children, ages 12, 9, and 5; their five-year-old niece; and a fifty-nine-year-old maternal grandmother. Laura at twelve years of age is the oldest, the adolescent in the family. She is tall, physically somewhat developed, and an outspoken central figure in the family.

Roberto, the father, is 45 years old, the oldest of two siblings. (His younger brother lives in Guatemala.) He is short and brown-skinned with small, delicate features. Extremely slender and wiry, he wears a perpetual furrow on his brow. Roberto was a journalist in Guatemala, born in the colonial capital of Antigua and raised since the age of one in Guatemala City.

Roberto's mother was of Italian ancestry, and Roberto remembers her as a very caring person. Her side of the family was "united." Roberto's mother's death fifteen years ago seems to have affected him deeply.

Roberto's father, Raúl, the paternal grandfather who was staying with the family for a brief period, is still an active influence on the family.

Raúl was at one time a prominent businessman in Guatemala City; through him, Roberto has connections to the United States. Raúl's father was a Texan with an American surname, which the family has inherited. That side of the family is very "disunited" according to Roberto. There is little family feeling due to many divorces and much bitterness. Other relatives of the father also seem to be mysteriously influential. Two uncles are involved in "legal matters." One works "for the U.S. government"; the other is a lawyer in Guatemala. "If there is a big problem, blood will still pull us together," states Roberto.

Roberto's background is apparently professional and middle class, bordering on elite. He has a baccalaureate degree from the University of San Carlos in science and letters, and he has worked as a professional journalist in newspapers and radio almost continually since 1960. In this work, Roberto covered politically sensitive national stories during recent times when events in Guatemala made such work dangerous. This included an interview with an ex-president of Guatemala that brought his journalism to public attention. Besides being as a journalist, Roberto has worked as a salesman at a number of odd jobs. He seems to be looking for ways to increase a still modest income.

Éster, his wife, is 41 years of age. She is short like her husband. Plump and vivacious, with broad Indian features, she darts around the home giving orders like a general and chastising her children constantly. Most noticeable is her round but nervous smile and her stream of stylish chatter. Éster is the oldest of two siblings; her twenty-five-year-old sister is still in Guatemala.

Éster was born in the Department of Totonicapán in central Guatemala; she lived in Sololá until she was five. After that, she was *internada*, or put in boarding schools, for most of her childhood. This experience, a common practice for families of all social classes in Guatemala (especially in the past) meant that she did not see her family except on vacations. After fifteen years of this type of education, she received a commercial certificate as a secretary-typist. When she found that she could not get a good job with this background, she went back to school in 1962 in order to get a teaching credential. She finally began her career as an elementary public school teacher in 1964 and worked continually in this profession until 1981, when she came to the United States.

Éster's mother, Beatriz de Ávila, is the maternal grandmother of the children, and she is the cook and children's caretaker in the home. Tall and light-skinned, she has an air of entitlement and past glories. During my visits, she regaled me with stories of her life in Guatemala as the wife of a military lieutenant. She said that she had traveled with her husband

and learned to shoot a pistol at a young age; she was a good marks-woman and horseback rider, too. Her family was of German ancestry, coming to Guatemala at the turn of the century. She also proudly showed me a treasured photograph of her own mother, a curly-headed blonde who was Miss Guatemala in the early 1900s. Éster, her daughter, has straight dark hair and dark eyes; she did not inherit the blonde curls.

The Decision to Move

In talking to members of the Walter family, I found that each individual had a slightly different version as to why the family decided to emigrate. No one in the family could be persuaded to make a definitive statement about the decision made as a family; rather, in Roshomon fashion, each constructed the story somewhat differently.

The father, Roberto Walter, told me that low salaries make it impossible for people to survive in Guatemala these days. He said that the general state of violence with people being shot dead in the streets had an unsettling effect on him. A number of his journalist friends had left the country before he decided to go. Many went to Mexico, Argentina, and Cuba. He said that there was a certain amount of risk in being a journalist now, even though he believed that the journalist was supposed to arrive only after the bullets had stopped flying. He made a strong attempt to impress me that he had not really been afraid for himself, but that the situation in general was bad. He did mention death threats that other journalists had received, and he said that he himself had received some back in 1975-1976. But, he said, he had not been concerned about this, and he continued his commentaries without being bullied by such telephone calls. Much of Roberto's conversation with me was in a very low voice as though he did not want his wife and mother-in-law to hear what he was saying. (They were in the next room.)

Mr. Walter said that his wife's teaching was a dangerous job too and that schoolteachers were often shot indiscriminately, not for anything that they were teaching but just because they were teaching people to read. He said that death could occur anywhere and anytime and that no one knows what will happen. In essence, Mr. Walter stressed to me that his concern was for the danger to his family as innocent bystanders; he came to the United States for the safety and protection of his wife and children.

Mrs. Walter told me that low salaries and the fighting between members of the government and the left had led her to wish to leave the country. She said that the decision was really Roberto's but that she had agreed, especially because she knew that he didn't want to stay in the

United States alone without his family. While Roberto had not been enthusiastic about coming, Éster said that she was quite sold on the plan. She stated that it was clearly the opportunity of a lifetime and that she had been blessed with much good fortune. While her husband was telling me that the plan was for the family to stay here only temporarily, for about five years, and then to return, Éster was sure that they would stay. Éster's vision was the old-fashioned American dream of progress; she also wanted to help out her husband so he wouldn't be alone.

Laura, the adolescent daughter, was not consulted about coming to the United States. Initially, she told me, she was very unhappy about the idea. She thought she would find no friends here. Happily, as with her mother, this turned out not to be the case, so she is now quite content to stay.

As for Beatriz, Éster's mother, her version of the emigration was somewhat different from any of the others. Doña Beatriz insisted that it was she who was responsible for bringing Éster and the girls to the United States. She told me that Éster didn't want to come, that she was afraid of learning English, and that she (Beatriz) had to talk her into it. Now, she noted, Éster had turned completely around and was pleased to be here. Beatriz herself told an interesting story of her dreams to come to the United States. She said that she had always admired the United States and had wanted to come here a long time ago. She had a woman friend who had come here and built up an undergarment factory and invited her to come and stay with her in Los Angeles many years ago. At that time, she said, although she and her husband were still married, she was separated from him and was looking around for opportunities. Another friend offered her $1,000 to come to New York and help her run an international gourmet restaurant. She had turned down both of her friends because she reconciled with her husband. This time, when Roberto left for California, Beatriz recognized that this would be her final chance to see the United States before she died. Now that she is here, though, she is quite homesick for Guatemala; she writes endless letters to her women friends there and tells anecdotes of her life back home over and over. She says that she does not want to go back to live there, though, because she is a widow and her family is here.

Clearly, a variety of factors were involved in the decision of the Walter family to come to the United States. Both Roberto and Éster were concerned about the worsening situation in Guatemala with regard to economics, politics, and violence. But in talking to the family about it, I found that they skirted around the decision-making issue in a very slippery manner, with no one taking responsibility for making the decision or for being the reason behind it (except for Beatriz). Instead, they tended to attribute the decision to other family members, as if it were shameful to take on such responsibility. This is partly a matter of cultural style in which polite conversation dictates that one circle around the point one wishes to make rather than making a forward and direct statement. But it also demonstrated something about this family's general decision-making process in which secret alliances seem to be made (for example, that between the mother and grandmother and that between the father and adolescent daughter) for particular goals. It appears to be inappropriate (or perhaps dangerous) for anyone to exert leadership in an obvious way in this family. I will explore this later in the section on the adolescent and family culture.

The central family figure in terms of opportunity, however, is the paternal grandfather, Raúl. He sent Roberto $250, and Roberto's cousin gave him some more money. Raúl had come to the United States in 1978 or 1979 and had obtained permanent residency because his father was an American. Thus, Roberto had the notion that, if needed, his father could petition for legal residency for Roberto and then for Roberto's family under the family reunification portion of immigration law. However, this did not come to pass. Raúl had a falling out with his daughter-in-law and her mother when they all arrived. He then refused to help in petitioning for them. He had his own troubles, too. His second wife had left him, and he had had a serious eye operation. For this reason he was staying with the Walter family for a brief period. There was a lot of tension in the home, however, due to the lack of resolution with regard to legal family reunification. Roberto Walter stated that his father and wife's family would work things out eventually with regards to U.S. residency. At the same time, he reiterated plans for all of them to return to Guatemala. When I pointed out that they might not wish to go, he said he would return "by myself, if necessary."

The Journey and Settling In

Roberto Walter came to the United States in September 1980 on a special visa, and the rest of the family came later. He came with a group of athletic judges for some international boxing matches. This was all arranged for him by one of his uncles with *cuello*.[2] The only problem was that his airline ticket was to Los Angeles, so his father had to fly there to bring him up to the San Francisco Bay Area. He then stayed with his father and found work parking cars and doing janitorial work. He was then able to save money to send home to help pay for the passages for his wife and daughters.

Back in Guatemala, Éster was also working to bring together the

$4,000 it took to pay for the passage for herself and her daughters. In addition to the money Roberto sent, she sold all the furniture in the house and took all of their savings out of the bank to pay the travel agency that arranged the move. Éster feels that they had very good luck in the whole experience, and she is quite pleased with how it all went. She said that a neighbor of hers was a friend of the owner of a travel agency. The travel agency owner had a secretary who was a friend of the U. S. consul. Therefore, Éster was able to arrange her family's visas with no problems whatsoever. They didn't even have to have an interview like Roberto had. All she needed to do was have enough money to show the embassy that she had the capacity to travel as a tourist. For this, she borrowed $10,000 from one of Roberto's cousins. This money was sent back to him immediately upon her arrival in the United States. Éster and her three children flew directly to San Francisco in April 1981.

When the family first arrived in the Bay Area, they came to stay with Raúl, their father-in-law, and his relatively new wife. By all accounts, this was a horrible experience for everyone. They lived in a tiny studio apartment in a complex where no children were allowed. Raúl and his wife felt encumbered and unhappy with the sudden increase of boarders (an increase of six, including four children). Beatriz clashed with them almost instantly, and the new arrivals were forced to leave the apartment every morning quite early and wander around in the parks and on the streets so the apartment manager would not become suspicious of their presence. This arrangement lasted for five months until Roberto finally located a small bungalow that the family was able to rent. During this period of time, while she was walking on the streets, Éster met some people who asked her if she wanted to babysit. So she began earning some money this way.

The home the Walter family now occupies is a small two-bedroom house. It is modest but neatly kept, with mementoes of Guatemala (a small flag, an insignia, a picture book) displayed on the walls. The family is quick to point out that it is not as nice as the home they had in Guatemala. Their home was larger there, with three bedrooms, lots of closet space, a garage, living and dining rooms, garden, balconies, fruit trees, and so on. They paid only $75 per month in house payments on it, as opposed to the $500 per month rent they pay here. But now the Guatemala home is being rented out and they are getting $125 monthly for it, so they are making $50 monthly. The family as a whole doesn't care much for the neighborhood they live in now compared to their *colonia* back home. In Guatemala, everyone in the neighborhood was friends; here, they don't know who their neighbors are. In general, they feel uncomfortable here in a heavily African-American community and with some Puerto Rican neighbors who drink too much fight, and yell a lot. The main problem, though, is that they don't know English.

The family gives mixed reactions to other aspects of life in the Bay Area. They are pleased with the schools for their younger girls, but Laura's middle school worries them. They feel that there is too much drug taking, and loose morality, and not enough control of the behavior of these adolescents. They also feel the work is too easy for Laura. She is doing extremely well and has even been moved up a grade so that she (at age 12) is in classes with 13- and 14-year olds. The parents feel that Guatemalan education is definitely superior to what they have found here. Laura herself is quite happy in the United States and has no wish to return to Guatemala except to visit. She has a peer group composed mainly of other Latinas, many of whom are Guatemalan. She also has Japanese and "American" friends.

Laura's ambition is to be a preacher in the Pentecostal church. She knows of a Pentecostal college in Los Angeles that she would like to attend. She also is interested in being a language teacher, fitting with her strengths in language and music. Laura is quite active socially at school and in her church youth group. Her mother says she is on the telephone all the time. Friends of hers celebrate *quinceñeros* and Laura would like to do the same when she turns 15, but doesn't know if the family will be able to afford it. Laura seems to keep quite busy with after-school sports activities and her church club, as well as another club that seems to be somewhat akin to the Girl Scouts. She says she is not interested in boys except for the popular Puerto Rican singing group Menudo.

The Walter family has not been in good health since their emigration. Nor are they pleased with the health care that is available in the United States. Everyone in the family with the exception of Éster has had lots of health problems since arriving in the San Francisco Bay Area. They blame a lot of it on the extremes of weather that they are not accustomed to. They miss "the eternal spring" for which Guatemala is famous. The whole family has suffered regular bouts of flu, bronchitis, and stomach aches. Beatriz has high blood pressure and phlebitis. She also claims that Éster is diabetic, but Éster denies this. Roberto had an accident in a parking lot where he was working; he fell and broke his ankle. He lost the job after he went to the County Hospital and the social worker reported the injury to workmen's compensation. The family also told me that doctors in the hospital rushed them through treatment, confused one of their daughters with another child, and (the grandmother feels) overprescribed medication that was "too strong" (for her heart condition). In the end, Roberto went to the University of

California Hospital in San Francisco for treatment for his ankle, since he was dissatisfied with the service in the County Hospital. Beatriz, the grandmother, takes charge of caring for the children when they are sick. She avoids doctors herself and feels she can help the family best with home remedies, many of which she says are Indian and very efficacious.

Éster has had good luck in finding work, she says. She cleans houses and has found her employers by walking through the wealthiest districts and putting little cards advertising her services in people's mailboxes. All of her employers have been good, she says; they have given her furniture and clothes and have treated her like a friend, not a servant. She turned to housecleaning from babysitting because it paid more. She worked for a while as a dishwasher in a Mexican restaurant, but she quit because they lowered her salary when the owner went on vacation.

Roberto was more mysterious about his work history. Although he went into much detail telling me about his professional jobs in Guatemala, he seemed to have a difficult time talking about the unskilled jobs he is taking here. Apparently, they range from janitor to parking lot attendant to managing a laundromat to working in a hot dog factory. (One time, after he told me that he had to go to work, his youngest daughter confessed to me in a low voice and in English, "My father doesn't have a job.") Another issue that arose was that Roberto had an alcohol problem. He told me that he had begun drinking to excess in Guatemala "after the earthquake" and that it got pretty bad in 1978 and 1979. He joined Alcoholics Anonymous for a year, and then he came to the United States. Four months after he arrived, he began drinking again, "but just beer." He has been drinking ever since, and it is starting to create a good deal of family friction.

Church is the one bright spot in the family's life. Roberto shopped around for a church when he got here and settled upon the Pentecostal church that they all now attend. Back in Guatemala the whole family had been Catholic, but they joined the Pentecostal church in 1979. Roberto said it was because they saw the need for a change, that they didn't like the way that Catholic priests got mixed up in politics. The family actually had begun the shift initially by involving themselves in the charismatic Catholic movement, a spiritual revitalization movement within the Catholic church. Then they made the move to the Pentecostal church. It is interesting to note that this also corresponds to Roberto's worst period of drinking, his cessation, and his joining of Alcoholics Anonymous. In any case, now the whole family is active in the local Pentecostal church which ministers to the Latin American population of the area. Church activities take up much of the family's limited free time, including three nights a week for women's group, young people's group, and a special class that Éster proudly teaches—Spanish for Latin Americans. In this class she teaches them how to be literate in their native tongue. Spanish language illiteracy is a serious problem, she feels, for many Latinos who are expatriates here in the United States. Roberto is the only one who is not wholeheartedly enthusiastic about the church, saying that he puts up with it but that he doesn't like its overemphasis on giving the church money. Here, people watch too much to see what you put into the collection plate, not like back in Guatemala.

The Adolescent and Family Culture

The two main themes in this family's culture appear to be success (*éxito*) and sacrifice (*sacrificio*). The Walters are very oriented toward the need to progress, to be able to buy American things and achieve recognition in the United States. Laura seems to carry many of the hopes of the family. Her parents are very supportive of her educational goals, and they are very proud of her achievements. But there is a sad side to the family, too. The Walters suffer a great deal in terms of their health and nurturance needs. The father, Roberto, is drinking excessively in bars and he and his wife are drifting more and more apart. When I came to interview them, the family was quite worried because Roberto had stayed away from home for several nights at a time. This pattern had occurred in Guatemala, as well, but the family had managed to cope with it through a religious conversion. Now the ideology is no longer enough. Here, too, Laura seems to be playing an important role. Roberto told me that he was trying to cut down on his drinking "because Laura doesn't like it. People start hitting each other and it gets bad."

The family has suffered a variety of physical ailments since arriving in the United States. Several family members have trouble sleeping at night. Beatriz, the grandmother, has a heart condition, high blood pressure, phlebitis, and other problems. Everyone else has had lots of colds and flu. The family also exhibited to me what bordered on abusive behavior toward the younger children. Éster sometimes locked them in the bedrooms and hit them with belts. They were only rarely allowed outdoors to play. Although I never saw any bruises, the belt was ever-present. Worries and fears seem to be taken out on each other, and somatic symptoms have appeared. Laura stated that when she had a stomach ache she feared it was an ulcer, like that of her father. (Her father never told me about his ulcer.)

The Walter family exhibits internal contradictions that are quite typical of Guatemala. Ethnically, the family has a dominating European overlay and a very subordinate Indian identity. Part of the family (the mother's side) is of military background with access to money and power. The rest of the family (the father's side) is ideologically moderately left-wing. The father stated (to me, quietly) that he was for a return of the Arévalo-Arbenz style of democracy (1944-1954) in Guatemala. The two sides of the family are covertly at war, making the family culture a microcosm of the tragically torn homeland they have left behind.

The one thing that the family clearly agrees on is the need for achievement. All members are enthusiastic about the necessity to work hard, acquire as much money as possible, and improve their living standard. In terms of the Moos Family Environment Scale, the Walter family falls into the achievement-oriented (with conformity) cluster. Their highest scores as a family are in achievement, moral-religious emphasis, and conflict. Their lowest scores are in independence, active-recreational orientation, and cohesion (see Figure 3).[3]

Achievement and religion appear to be vehicles through which the family is attempting to both reconcile opposing ideologies and develop some self-esteem. This strategy has been most successful for the mother, grandmother, and adolescent daughter. Laura, in addition, has her good school record to boost her own and the family's morale. The mother, Éster, has managed to reestablish herself as a teacher in the church setting and thus is receiving recognition if not financial reward. But the father, Roberto, is definitely floundering in his work identity. Downward mobility (and inability to work for a time due to an injury to his ankle) has hurt his self-esteem immeasurably, and he deals with this by drinking excessively. (Ironically, he dislikes the Mexican cantinas and refuses to frequent any but American and Italian bars.) Such a state of affairs has increased family tension and conflict. Beatriz, the grandmother, has attempted to build her sense of achievement by taking on a leadership position in the family, allying with her daughter, Éster. This has meant disastrous results for the marital pair of husband and wife. A vicious cycle is in process—of attempted overcompensation on the part of the entire family, withdrawal and drinking by the father when he fails to achieve everyone's high expectations, and more involvement of by the grandmother. Father, then, finds only Laura to be a nonjudgmental support. The primary coalitions in the family are Éster and Beatriz, and Roberto and Laura.

There is not an inordinate amount of disagreement about the family culture among family members. The family incongruence score on the Moos scale (see Figure 3) is 16, which is about average.

In terms of cohesion and adaptability, the family presents itself as "rigidly disengaged," with Éster (mother) and Laura (adolescent) desiring "chaotic separation."[4] That is, both mother and daughter feel quite

FIGURE 3 - The Walter Family

Family Environment Scale

(FES)

Family Incongruence Score = 16

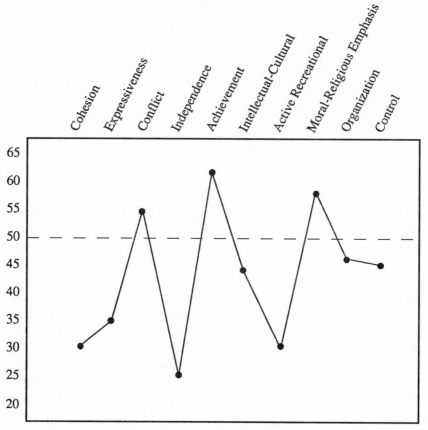

hemmed in (perhaps by the rigidity of grandmother and father) and want no organizational structure to hold them back. What they feel held back from is adaptability—in their terms, achievement, success (*éxito*). In the process of fighting to attain it, many sacrifices (*sacrificios*) have been made, and much pain is evident in the family as a result. Mother and daughter would like to be slightly more bonded as a family—separated instead of totally disengaged, according to the Olson FACES test (see Figure 4).

Laura, the adolescent, is attempting to reconcile the conflict by taking on the ambitious role of moral leader for the family. It was she who referred them once for family counseling, and her ambition is to be a preacher. She is the only one in the family who seems to have both sides in the battle listening to her and respecting her opinions. This is heady responsibility for a girl of 12, but it is a common situation for many immigrant families. Notably, this family conflict carries the particular cultural and historical mark of Guatemalan ethnic, social, and political contradictions that were discussed in earlier sections of this book.[5]

Control y Libertad—Desesperando: The Chavez Family

Origins

I first encountered the Chavez family through their adolescent son Ernesto, whom I met at a high school for immigrants in San Francisco. He told me that he lived with his twenty-one-year-old brother. When pressed, he acknowledged that his father also lived with him. When I contacted his father, I found that this youth was part of a large family that was gradually coming to the United States from Guatemala.

The total family consists of the husband, the wife, and their eleven children. José Chavez is the sixty-one-year-old father and titular head of household in San Francisco. Seven of his children are also living in San Francisco; they range in age from 16 (Ernesto) to 31. These seven children are Inez, 31; María, 28; José, 25; Rosa, 23; Gustavo, 21; Dolores, 19; and Ernesto, 16. The four oldest children are married, and Inez and Rosa have young children of their own. Still in Guatemala are Natalia Chavez (the mother) and the four youngest children, who range in age from eight to fifteen.

At the point that I began to interview the family, they were all living together in two households. One was in an African-American ghetto neighborhood; the other was in the heavily Latino Mission district.

FIGURE 4 - The Walter Family

Family Adaptability and Cohesion Scale
(FACES)

Family Discrepancy Score = 14.8

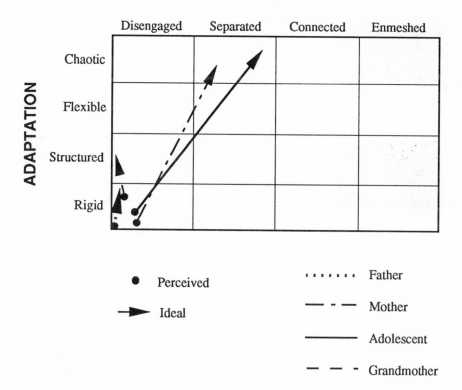

COHESION

| | Disengaged | Separated | Connected | Enmeshed |

ADAPTATION

Chaotic

Flexible

Structured

Rigid

● Perceived

→ Ideal

· · · · · · Father

— · — Mother

——— Adolescent

— — - Grandmother

During the eight-month period in which I interviewed pertinent family members, the family further divided into two additional households, and some shifting of membership took place. Because of the complex living arrangements and because of the difficulty I had in finding many of the family members to be available for interviewing, I concentrated on interviewing (mostly individually) only three family members in this study: the father, José Chavez; his sixteen-year-old son, Ernesto; and his nineteen-year-old daughter, Dolores. Also, because of the limited educational background of the family and their embarrassment about lack of sophistication with such instruments, the pencil-and-paper family evaluation tests were not given.

José Chavez is a small man with definite Indian features. He has a puckish smile and wears a straw hat. His home is a small village in the Department of San Marcos, the westernmost area of Guatemala, bordering on Chiapas, Mexico. Mr. Chavez was born in 1922 in a tiny border town near the Mexican frontier and was raised in a village that is farther inland. He is a Mam Indian, although he claims not to remember very much of the language. His mother was very poor, he says, but she had a small plot of land, five *manzanas*, which is still his today.

Mr. Chavez did not know his father, who died working in the fields when José was only one year of age. His mother alone raised her family—José and his two older brothers and sisters. His mother told him stories of her hard life, how she worked as a domestic in the kitchen and sold tortillas in the plaza in order to make a living. When he was eight years old, he was sent away to school (*internado*). He was able to complete only the third grade, having to drop out at the age of 12 in order to go to work. He was the one in the family who was to care for his mother. They lived on her land and raised corn, wheat, potatoes, and beans. He became rebellious and at a young age began to drink (*chupear*) and to party (*parandear*), much to his mother's dismay. When he was 16, he made a big change and, along with his mother and many others in his town, became an evangelical Christian. He did this because he noticed that those people who were "recognizing the Lord" were leading more sober and honest lives. Mainly, they didn't drink. At this time, therefore, he gave up his misspent youth, converted, and started to work again. These were hard years. He had to work along with his mother on their own land, but he also had to work without wages on the large landowners' *fincas* for two months out of each year.

When Mr. Chavez was 20 years old, he was conscripted into the military. He served for a year and a half until 1944, when, owing to new opportunities (the change in government), he traveled to Guatemala City to work in construction for a year or two. There he encountered

Natalia, who was from his home village but was working in Guatemala City as a live-in domestic. Mr. Chavez returned to his village to take care of his mother; Natalia also returned, and they began to live together. Thus Mr. Chavez began his family. José and Natalia had six children together before they finally got married (José was 45, Natalia 40, when they got married). They had five more children before the family was complete. During this time living in San Marcos, José Chavez continued to grow corn, wheat, potatoes, and beans. He generally worked his own land for three to four months and then traveled to Mexico to work in the coffee plantations for two months out of each year. This was necessary to make money so that his children could go to school. Mexico was appealing because the salaries are higher there than in Guatemala.

In 1960 the government began to set up "cooperatives" for campesinos in the area where Mr. Chavez had his land. One cooperative, named Cooperative Justino Rufino Barrios, was established in which chemical fertilizer and seeds were given to the farmers to help them increase production. Mr. Chavez says that at first this cooperative was a big help. For three years they did well. Then things started to revert to the old bad situation. They began to charge for the fertilizer and seed and each year the prices got higher. At the same time, the crops were not commanding the earnings they had gotten before. The Chavez family was forced once again to engage in the migratory coffee plantation labor, which they had forsaken during the good times. This state of affairs has continued to the present day, only it has worsened. Campesinos bought fertilizer and seeds on credit for a while, but, like Mr. Chavez, many have had their credit lines closed. Mr. Chavez and his family have been left with thousands of dollars of debts now owed to the cooperative. These debts are a great burden for José and Natalia, especially with a family of eleven children.

The Decision to Move

According to José, after his wife delivered their last child in 1976, she became ill, and he had to take her to Guatemala City. It turned out that she had uterine cancer and had to have a hysterectomy. Since then, she has been weak and unable to work. Natalia's operation cost the family extra money and put an additional strain on the already difficult financial conditions that they were facing. Around this time, Rosa, their sixteen-year-old daughter and fourth-oldest child, came with the family to Guatemala City and found work as a live-in domestic. She worked for a family for a year or so. Then, when her employers chose to move to the United States, she went with them. This was in 1978. Rosa, at age 18, managed to save enough money in the United States to send remittances to her family along with stories about the beautiful life in the United States.

At this same time, conditions at home were becoming more and more critical for José and his family. They were finding it impossible to get credit any more, and the debt collectors from the cooperative were beating on their door. They were charging exorbitant interest rates on the loans the family had taken out; they were threatening to take the family's home and to jail Mr. Chavez. While these events were occurring, political organizers from the Christian Democratic and Liberation parties began to operate in the area, getting people involved in the political process. Many of the campesinos joined the parties. Lots of promises were made. Mr. Chavez himself became active in the Christian Democratic party. He said that a lot of people knew him, and he was in a strong position to help mobilize the people of his village.

Suddenly, says Mr. Chavez, political candidates for office began to be murdered. There were disappearances, kidnapping, and torturing of people who had been involved in political activities. Especially singled out were schoolteachers, doctors, and the directors of the cooperative. In 1979, Mr. Chavez's daughter Inez left for the United States. She joined Rosa, and both of them sent remittances to help support the family. Mr. Chavez became even more fearful when the violence grew to the proportions of war in 1980. Government helicopters were burning and destroying neighboring villages and crops. Guerilleros and government soldiers were fighting. It was impossible to know who was who, so people suffered fear and mistrust.

Although José Chavez had been thinking of coming north for a long time, the opportunity to do so had not presented itself. He did not have the money. In addition, Natalia did not want to be left behind; she wanted to come also. So José Chavez waited even though he was receiving threats about his debts. Finally, in 1980, the family amassed enough capital from children in the United States to finance the trip—first for José, the son, age 22, and a few months later for José, the father, and Gustavo, then age 17.

The last four members of the Chavez family to enter the United States came in 1982, at the height of the border violence. First came María (then age 27) and her eighteen-year-old sister Dolores. They crossed over in May. In November, fifteen-year-old Ernesto came with an uncle. In all cases, the older brothers and sisters financed and set up the trips.

Until recently, the Chavez family has had as its operating plan the process of bringing family members north from Guatemala one or two at a time every few months or years until, gradually, all of them are here. Rosa began the chain migration, and it has been a family project for each new arrival to aid the next family member to come. However, events and circumstances have made these family dreams difficult to fulfill. In 1982 the Department of San Marcos was the scene of a great deal of terrorism and destruction. Even working on the family land plot became too dangerous for the remaining Chavez family members because of crop burning and helicopter sweeps. Thus, the migration process accelerated. The last emigration was in 1982 when four family members came north. Since then, there have been a number of hardships and difficulties for family members in the United States, and the operating assumption—that of bringing the entire family up one or two at a time—has been called into question.

Both adolescents in the family (Ernesto, who is now 16 and Dolores, now 19) were highly in favor of the emigration. Ernesto saw it as a chance to continue his schooling. He knew that he could not continue at home, that he would have to work. He saw it as an unequivocal opportunity to accomplish dreams he would never be able to achieve back in Guatemala. When I interviewed Ernesto about his immigration experience, he held back on telling me anything of the terrorist conditions that had led to his family's exodus. Still, the strength of his determination to stay in this country was unshakable. Throughout the interview, Ernesto appeared to be quite tense. He nervously tore apart a paper cup and made a series of deep dents in an unopened can of evaporated milk with one bare hand. These movements contrasted sharply with the calmness and understatement with which he answered many of my questions.

Dolores also stated matter-of-factly that life is very difficult at home now and that she wanted to come to the United States to satisfy "*una ilusión a conocer otro lugar*" (a dream to know another place). However, Dolores had another, unacknowledged (but perhaps more compelling reason) to leave home and come to the United States. Dolores is the unwed mother of a year-old baby. The story finally came out. At home in her village, Dolores had a relationship for three to four years with a young man whom she loved and admired. He was kind and decent, she felt, unlike other men. They had considered marriage. But Dolores began to notice that he was starting to go with other women. Dolores felt that she should leave him, so she told him that she was going to go to Guatemala City to work. No matter, he told her; he, too, was going to Guatemala City with some friends, and they would see each other there. She did not tell him that she was really planning to come to the

United States.

Dolores's story to me was that she did not realize she was pregnant until she was on her way to the United States. However, since the baby was born full-term in October, she had to have been four months pregnant before she left home in May. As she noticed the usual first trimester symptoms of pregnancy (nausea and fluctuations in appetite, breast tenderness, and missed menstrual cycles), it seems likely, despite her denial, that at least at some somatic level, Dolores was aware of her dilemma before she left Guatemala. Dolores told me that unwed motherhood is not well accepted in her village. "People either blame the man or the woman." It seems likely, then, that Dolores's coming to the United States at that time was fortuitous if not (as she says) related to the pregnancy. In any case, Dolores wrote to the baby's father informing him of the birth of the baby. At first he wrote back and denied paternity. Later, however, in another letter, he recognized the child and suggested that Dolores return to Guatemala so that they could marry. Dolores says she will not do this. She says that she has no way of knowing if he might change his mind by the time she gets there. Besides, it is an expensive trip with too many risks. She feels she can do better to take her chances here in the United States.

The father of the family, the elder José Chavez, carries the indelible memory of the "push" factors that impelled the family to become both labor migrants and refugees. Although he spoke to me in an understated tone (due to cultural style), the facts he related spoke for themselves: The family was forced to leave. While his adolescent children also expressed themselves in the same reserved style, they held back even more. As the younger generation, they are denying a past that they do not want to remember. Instead, they want to see themselves as immigrants (this is interpreted as positive connotation) rather than refugees (negative connotation), and they focus on the "pull" factors that give them a vision for their future. Ernesto's dreams for a good education and Dolores's choice to risk single motherhood in the United States are future-oriented goals. It is significant that Dolores states now that she did not know she was pregnant before she left Guatemala. She is determined that the new baby will be a child of the United States and of the future, not of the past.

The Journey and Settling In

The Chavez family are peasant farmers; due to their rural geograph-ical origin and lack of resources, they had no recourse other than to enter the United States overland, or *mojado*.[6] Rosa is the only family member to enter another way; she was brought here by a Guatemala City family as a servant. Chavez family members who have come overland all came north with a *coyote* (people smuggler) along with a small group of other emigrants. Generally, it cost them $500 per day for the services of the *coyote,* which included hotels, meals, and bus transportation. Passing into Mexico from Guatemala was not difficult for them. It is quite easy to get a visa to enter Mexico, as many Guatemalans work in the coffee and other plantations of Mexico on a seasonal basis. The difficult part of the trip was the border crossing into the United States. For Mr. Chavez, it meant six days of nightmares in which he, Gustavo, and their companions hid in the mountains without food, waiting for their transportation to San Francisco. After he arrived in San Francisco, Mr. Chavez became ill from the difficult trip and was hospitalized with pneumonia for four days.

For Ernesto, the entire trip took four days and cost $2,000. Gustavo sent him the money, built up his courage, and arranged for the *coyote* with whom he traveled. He and his uncle made the trip together along with thirteen others. On the first day they crossed the Mexican border; on the second day they took a bus to Mexico City; on the third day they traveled to the U.S. border at San Luis. There they found an isolated spot at night, swam the Colorado River, and ran for several hours until they were safely away from the border guards. This last day was the most difficult part of the trip. But Ernesto was convinced that even if they were caught by the immigration police, he would claim to be Mexican and would be back the next day. In spite of his enthusiastic attitude about the journey, however, Ernesto did admit that the experience was very hard on him. He said that he had never had an experience that was so wearing and so full of fears and unknowns.

Dolores speaks of her experience coming to the United States as if she were in a dream. Although she recalled that her brother Gustavo paid $900 total to a *coyote* to bring her up directly along with her sister Maria, she seems able or willing only to recall or relate that things worked out well, that God watched over her and gave her good luck. She told me that the entire trip was made by auto and that she was asleep during the crossing of the U.S. border. She seems unable to explain how she was able to get across the frontier traveling in a car without any legal documents. The most she would tell me was that the Mexican *coyote* knew his way around. From my contact with Dolores it was unclear as to how much of her experience might have been blotted out of her memory. Her calm and dreamy story of the border crossing may be similar to her approach to her pregnancy, that of a covering up or repression of awareness of a painful reality. Was she drugged? She also may have been fearful and suspicious of me.

The Chavez family is connected to a wide network of Guatemalan migrants and refugees from the Department of San Marcos. After Rosa and Inez entered the United States in 1978 and 1979, a steady stream of family relations, friends, and acquaintances followed. Older arrivals helped newer arrivals, providing them food and shelter. Such reciprocity made finding housing somewhat easier for the large Chavez family, since friends would vacate their apartments and houses and pass them on.

Through such contacts, the Chavez family was able to find a suitable home. Located in a black neighborhood of San Francisco, it now appears to function as a domicile for Rosa, her husband, and their two children, and as a center for new arrivals. All Chavez family members have lived in this home when they first arrived. Rosa and Inez seem to have been in charge of the organization of the household.

After some time living together, the four oldest married adult children went their separate ways. First Inez and her husband and baby daughter moved to the Mission district. Then José (the son) and his wife found their own apartment. Finally, María rented a fourth apartment also in the Mission district. (María's husband is still in Guatemala; Dolores traveled with her to the United States and moved in with her in her new apartment.) Following the dispersal of the married adult children, the two other unmarried brothers, Gustavo and Ernesto, moved in with their sister Inez. José Chavez, the father, began to move among the various homes, staying with different adult children for brief periods and then moving on.

The living situation for the family in San Francisco is now quite a contrast to the ambience they experienced back home in San Marcos. As campesinos (peasant farmers), the family members were rural Ladinoized Indians. Their home in Guatemala was out in the country and was separated by a great distance from other homes. It was adobe, with an earthen floor. There was a little structure right next to the house where the animals were kept. They had no electricity; instead, they used candles and a gas lamp. They cooked with firewood and had to heat water to bathe. Here, they are impressed with the ease of light switches, with the bathrooms, and especially the wall-to-wall carpets in the homes and apartments they rent. They appreciate the conveniences, but they also note that in Guatemala their home was more elegant than their neighbors' homes, that the weather was milder, and that there was no need for a heating system such as they need here in the Bay Area. Here, in comparison with the housing that is generally available, their apartments are not in such good condition and maintenance is very expensive. The Chavez family members show evidence of much resilience; they have adapted well to all these changes. In one home, I noted a striking example of integration of the old and familiar with the new: In one corner of a bedroom was a sheet that had been attached to the walls to form a hammock. Next to it was a Sony Walkman stereo radio.

There is only one member of the family who is attending school full-time. Ernesto is in the ninth grade in a large urban high school. He started out attending a special high school designed for immigrant students, but after a semester he was transferred to the school he now attends. In addition to his studies, Ernesto works as a dishwasher in a restaurant five days a week, six hours a day. Ernesto says he is doing well, having no problems, but he is bewildered by the great numbers of students who cut classes and do not seem to take their studies seriously. Ernesto has to bus across town to get to school, but he does not see this as a hardship because he had to walk long distances to school in Guatemala. He is getting "good marks" in mathematics and art. English is his biggest problem. Having been in the United States for less than a year, he feels that once he learns English, everything else will follow. Ernesto has ambitions to be a medical doctor. He does not express any well-formulated plan as to how he intends to accomplish this, nor does he seem to appreciate the numerous obstacles in his path. He is optimistic, hard-working, and goal-directed. His family is proud of him.

The Chavez family has had several experiences with the health resources of San Francisco. José Chavez was hospitalized with pneumonia after he arrived. Dolores gave birth to her baby in the County Hospital, and a month later Gustavo was hit by a bus and was seriously injured. Finally, Mr. Chavez sought the services of the dental clinic for some reconstructive work. (He did not complete the work, however, as he ran out of money.) In all instances, the family was very pleased with the care that they received. Dolores attended some postpartum baby care classes at the hospital and was quite taken with a Spanish-speaking nurse who took an interest in her and her baby. Gustavo received excellent inpatient and outpatient care for his extensive internal and external injuries, and he is presently recuperating at home. Mr. Chavez's only complaint about the dental work was that it was taking too long and costing too much.

The Chavez family is affiliated with a small but active evangelical Pentecostal church in the Mission district. The congregation is practically all Central American, and it is quite small and socially interconnected. Although all family members belong to the church, they seem to go to meetings and services individually since they live apart and have different schedules. Dolores, the adolescent daughter, does not like the church

as much as the one she attended in Guatemala. She does not approve
of all the noise made about "speaking in tongues." The church at home
was more proper, she thinks. The evangelical church in the neighborhood serves some very important functions for this family. Through
gossip, it provides a mechanism for social connectedness and control. It
also is a hotline for information about available work for the new
arrivals. Some of the elders in the church are labor contractors with
construction firms. They have a ready supply of labor in their congregation. Mr. Chavez found most of his jobs through contacts in the church.

Work is the major concern of the Chavez family here in the United
States. All of the females and the younger males work as dishwashers
in a number of Mexican and Italian restaurants. They generally work
from the late afternoon to late at night, six days a week, but on different
days. On days off, family members help out by taking care of the babies.
(There are four little girls, ranging from one to three years of age.) The
older males (José, Jr. and Sr., plus the husbands of Rosa and Inez) work
in construction, painting houses, or *sandblasteando* (sandblasting). A
portion of each person's earnings goes to a common fund for household
expenses; another portion goes back to Guatemala; the final portion may
be kept by each individual. A big change for the Chavez family was
noted by José, Sr. Back in Guatemala he and his wife made all the
decisions about the household jointly. Here, he says, the older daughters
are in charge. They buy everything and pay all the bills.

Mr. Chavez was adamant that unless he was working regularly here
in the Bay Area, he was just wasting time. Mostly, he wanted to work
in construction, but he would take any work. The jobs he got were few
and far between. He told me that he was concerned because in the past,
when he worked as a labor migrant in Mexico, he lost his direction and
reverted to drinking and other vices. When he has a lot of free time, it
there is more opportunity for him to get into trouble. Mr. Chavez was
being realistic about his problem, for as a 61-year-old, non-English-
speaking Indian farmer, his services are not much in demand in the Bay
Area urban marketplace. Throughout my interviews with him, he
expressed continuing worry about this situation and stated clearly that he
would leave the area if he could not locate some regular work soon. He
mused about traveling to the Salinas Valley or to San Diego to pick
strawberries and do similar work. He had heard that there was work
from some Salvadorans he had met. Finally, though, as I completed the
interviewing process, he had decided to return to Guatemala when he
learned that his wife was ill again.

I interviewed Mr. Chavez shortly after the most recent coup by Mejía
Victores over Ríos Montt (in August 1983). This was four months

before Mr. Chavez returned to Guatemala. At the time of that interview, Mr. Chavez was concerned about the repercussions of the coup on his village and his family. He told me that he received news that things were very bad there, that prices were soaring, and that, as a result, many people were being victimized by bandits. He said that there was a new edict in the town that everyone must carry identification papers, including a birth certificate, on their person at all times. He said that people were so frightened that they did not leave their homes and thus could not make a living, go to the market to buy or sell food, or even leave the country for Mexico to escape. He said he heard that the border was guarded heavily and that labor migrants were no longer allowed to pass. He said that in all his life he had never heard of things getting as bad as they were now. He spoke of oppression and destruction of a country and of the "poor people" who are just trying to live.

On the other hand, Mr. Chavez's experiences since arriving in the United States have left him very disheartened. The year 1982 was particularly difficult for him. In this period, his last remaining sibling, a sister with whom he was very close, died of cancer in Guatemala. His son Gustavo was seriously injured in an accident and was recovering. Most important, it was proving to be impossible to make the money that he had anticipated he could make in the United States. All in all, Mr. Chavez felt he needed to return home. He also decided that Gustavo should come with him.

At the present time, Dolores and Ernesto are taking their chances on staying in the United States. They see opportunities, a vision of freedom and independence, and escape from oppression. But they are faced with a number of ominous liabilities such as psychic denial, accidents (like Gustavo's), and family conflict and division. Also, the family may now be permanently separated.

In my contacts with Dolores, she has generally looked depressed and deprived. She is missing three front teeth (they were pulled out by a dentist in San Marcos because they stuck out) and she usually looks disheveled (her hair is uncombed, etc.). She hardly leaves her apartment except to work. She is still struggling with her tentative plans for freedom (obtaining welfare and her own apartment), but she uses a lot of denial and fantasy. She is an addict of the television *novelas*, or Spanish soap operas. She has not tried to learn English.

When I first met Ernesto he was apparently ashamed of his father's rural manner and did not acknowledge that he lived with him. Now Ernesto is continuing to work hard to put his past behind him. With his heavy work and school schedule, he gets only about four hours of sleep a night; he is tired all the time. Nonetheless, one night after my interviewing was completed, I was surprised to see Ernesto at a very chic Spanish restaurant in San Francisco. He had finished working there for the evening, and he was dressed in evening attire complete with a dressy shirt unbuttoned somewhat provocatively. Ernesto has ambitions of marrying an American girl (from a list he hopes to find; he will be happy to pay) and establishing himself in the United States legally with all the associated privileges. He exhibits the confidence and winning naiveté that may yet carry him through this process, although in reality the obstacles to his dreams are indeed formidable.

The Adolescent and Family Culture

In this family, the central theme is that of freedom and control (*control y libertad*) and of losing hope (*desesperando*). It is exemplified in the two adolescents who are moving toward independence in their relationship to the family. For example, Ernesto has taken on the very ambitious goal of studying to be a physician, although he has not shared this idea with his family. Dolores had a baby outside of marriage, yet she has chosen to live in the United States as a single mother and is even applying for welfare, hoping to be able to live on her own with her baby.

There are striking contrasts in the brother's and sister's approach to independence, and in the attitudes and expectations of other family members toward each of them. The family expresses pride in and support of Ernesto. On the other hand, Dolores's very existence was not acknowledged by her father until the end of my second interview with him. They see her duty as that of worker and mother to her daughter. Beyond that, she is dealt with critically and as somewhat of an embarrassment.

I see this contrast to a great extent as a function of the rigid sex-role expectations that are an integral part of the Chavez family culture. The men in the family think that men should work and that they need to watch out for exposure to vices. The danger of such exposure increases when the family is engaged in labor migration because the family solidarity and cohesion (that is, the moral leadership of the wife) is missing. All kinds of things can happen, and Gustavo's accident is an indication that they do happen.

Proper women, on the other hand, are expected by the men of the family to wear dresses, care for their children, behave modestly, and need protection from the men. In the San Francisco setting, the men note with dismay that by working outside the home, women take over the running of the household and start to wear pants. For example, Dolores recognizes new opportunities. She sees she can be less dependent on her family if she receives welfare. Also, she covets a more sexual, less matronly look, and she dreams of dieting and attending an exercise class.

Another way in which the family culture struggles with freedom and control issues is in the contrast between the old Indian, rural Guatemalan refugee identity and the new Ladinoized, young immigrant identity. The old Indian identity symbolizes oppressive control to this family, but it also symbolizes family cohesion. As of the date of this writing, the father has returned to Guatemala because his wife became sick again, and Gustavo accompanied him. Although Mr. Chavez told me he would come back to the United States "in a few months," Ernesto and Dolores tell me it is likely that he will stay there. They have not heard how their mother is doing, but only that their father and Gustavo took her to Guatemala City to see a doctor there.

The gulf between the family's expectations of life in the United States and the reality they are facing is immense. Although the family tries to be optimistic and continues to work hard to achieve their goals, they are clearly losing ground. Their rural Indian experience and family left behind is so far from the urban "fast lane" as to defy understanding. Ernesto expects somehow to complete high school and go to medical school and become a physician. But the facts are that his English is extremely limited, he is 16 years old and in the ninth grade, he is not in the country legally, he has no financial resources to pay for such an undertaking, his own family is not aware of his plans, and he has not discussed these plans with any guidance counselor in his high school. Ernesto's fantasy is that he will be able to find an American girl to marry, thus pulling him into the mainstream of the American dream. Dolores has put great hopes on the financial gain she can achieve by receiving welfare. She is eligible because her child was born in the United States, but she will be faced with a good many other obstacles in terms of the bureaucracy itself. The image of her *novela* heroine Veronica who suffers for love in a Parisian original gown will not be something that her welfare budget can maintain. Finally, Mr. Chavez, the father, also had expectations about being able to find steady work in the United States and send home large remittances to his wife and family. Thus, even before his wife became ill, Mr. Chavez was *desesperando* (losing hope), and he finally decided to return home.

One dramatic psychological resolution of the dichotomy between freedom and control in this family can be seen in the recurring dreams reported to me by Ernesto. He tells me that at night he sees himself riding on horseback through the familiar countryside of Guatemala. In this dream, he resolves his need for freedom and security: He is free, and at home.

Asimilando—América y El Alma: The García Family

Origins

A former co-worker of mine, who is a community outreach worker with the county mental health program, told me that she knew a Guatemalan woman who was well acquainted with a number of Guatemalan families living in the San Francisco peninsula area. This woman referred me to the Garcías, a single-parent family headed by Juana García. Ms. García lives in the peninsula community of San Mateo with her two teenage daughters and eight-year-old son. She is 45 years old, is of working-class background, and has never married. Juana García is a light-skinned woman who looks a good deal older than her 45 years. She has gray hair and a care-worn expression. Her voice is tired and distinctively tremulous; it has the cadence of a much older person. Her adolescent daughters are Esperanza, who is 14, and Aurelia, 13. Esperanza is slender and serious with long, thick, curly black hair. Aurelia is chubby and has a fun-loving grin; she giggles a lot. Both girls dress fashionably. They were formal and nervously self-conscious in talking to me on my visits. The younger brother, Sergio, generally answers the door and the telephone. He appears to be outspoken and more at ease. At eight years of age, he seems accorded some deference as the only "man" in the house.

Ms. García was born in Mazatenango, which she says is a large and modern city in the Department of Suchitepequez on the southwestern coast of Guatemala. She is the fourth of six children. Her parents met while her mother was a cook and her father a baker. But the union did not last and her parents separated when Juana was three years old. Juana never saw her father again. Juana's mother moved her family from Mazatenango after she and Juana's father separated. They lived in Quetzaltenango for two years, and in 1944 they moved to Guatemala City. Juana's mother started her in a Catholic school run by nuns, but she had to remove her and transfer her to a public school after a year due to lack of funds for the tuition.

Juana stayed in school until she was 14 years old. After that she left school and began working to help out her mother. She worked cleaning houses and babysitting. Meanwhile, her mother had two additional children; Juana assisted with their care as well. Her main occupation for six or seven years of her youth was as a caretaker for an elderly paralytic woman. She also helped in caring for her grandmother, who by this time was old and sickly. Juana says that her grandmother wouldn't let anyone else take care of her but Juana.

Ms. García tired of this type of life when she was 19. She decided to strike out on her own. She set up a little refreshment concession and began looking for likely places to sell her wares. She ended up joining a traveling fair that moved throughout the southeastern part of Guatemala. In this way she met Felipe Hernandez, the father of her first two children; he also had a traveling refreshment business. For a time they combined their businesses, but they decided they could make more money if they diversified. Consequently, Juana set up a lottery concession next to his refreshment concession. Both businesses complemented each other.

This arrangement was satisfactory for a while. When Juana became pregnant with her first child at the age of 20, she returned to Guatemala City and her mother took care of the new baby. As time went by, Juana and Felipe's relationship soured, and Juana, pregnant again, returned to Guatemala City to live with her mother. Juana's two oldest children are the product of this liaison. They are Gloria, now age 24, and Manuel, now age 20. Both Gloria and Manuel are newly married with young children and are living in the San Mateo area.

Back in Guatemala City in 1964, Juana García looked to make a new start. She soon met another man, Sebastián Sotelo, who was also to cause her grief.

When I met him he told me that he was single, that he lived with his mother, and that he wanted to get together with someone. He was an auto mechanic with a good job and he helped me out. We had three children together [Esperanza, Aurelia, and Sergio]. Later I found out that he had a wife and fifteen children. This was very hard for me to take, especially with so many children. I found him out because one day he didn't return from work. I had started to suspect him because he often said he was at work when he really wasn't. I went looking for him at his workshop. They said that he had left. There was a young boy who was also working there; someone said that he lived with Mr. Sotelo. I decided to follow that boy and I knocked on the door of his home. A woman answered and I asked her if she was the wife of Mr. Sotelo. She said she was. I said, "Oh, I'm the wife of the man in charge of house repairs," or something like that. I didn't want her to know who I was. And then I left.

After Juana discovered how she had been deceived, she was very cold to Sebastián Sotelo, she said. Whenever he would come and try to make up to her, bringing presents and all, she would treat him as a stranger. So it was that he stopped coming back, and she was left alone with the children.

The Decision to Move

Juana had been thinking of coming to the United States ever since the birth of her second child, Manuel, when she was just 24 years old. Her younger sister, Marina, had come to the San Francisco Bay Area in the 1960s after hearing encouraging reports of life in the United States from a friend. Marina had established a "beachhead" here and a network of other Guatemalan friends and families with whom she was in contact. Periodically, Marina went back and forth between Guatemala and the United States as a labor migrant, leaving her daughter, Marilyn, behind in Guatemala when she came back to the United States to earn an income. On her visits to Guatemala she would tell Juana about how beautiful it is in the San Francisco area and how easy it is to make money. But Juana was inhibited from joining Marina because her mother objected. Her mother feared that she would never see Juana again. Juana felt that she was the person in the family most responsible for her mother, so she could not desert her.

In 1975, a number of events converged for Juana that made a trip to the United Sates appear inevitable. First, Juana's mother became ill and needed medical attention. Second, Juana, pregnant with her fifth child, discovered Sebastián Sotelo's deception. Finally, financial conditions were becoming more and more difficult for her. Juana had bought a house in Guatemala City, but she was finding it impossible to keep up with the payments. She received a letter advising her that $250 was due and payable on the house and that if she did not pay it immediately, she would lose the house. Moreover, unemployment was widespread in Guatemala City. "I would read in the paper about how many people were unemployed in Guatemala, and in another section of the paper there would be announcements of jobs with good salaries in the United States."

Juana was able to obtain a tourist visa, so she bought a plane ticket to San Francisco. She left five-year-old Esperanza and four-year-old Aurelia with a neighbor and flew to the United States to join Marina. At that time, her intention was to stay temporarily and to raise enough capital to both pay off her mother's medical bills and her house payments and to support her children. Juana managed to make her house payments, and then she took out a second mortgage and financed the trip to the United States for her oldest daughter, Gloria, whom she expected to help her. Gloria flew up on a tourist visa with Juana's sister, Marina.

The 1976 earthquake upset all of the plans. The four years following the quake were extremely difficult ones for Juana and her family. Ms. García returned home to find that Esperanza had been badly frightened by the quake; she suffered from *susto* and was unable to eat or talk for a while. Ms. García also gave birth to her last child, Sergio, a few months after her return. The house was ruined, too, and Juana was obliged to supervise its reconstruction. Furthermore, Juana was assigned by the local Catholic church to distribute emergency food supplies to her neighborhood. (Her previous business experience in running a refreshment and lottery concession had made her well respected in the area.)

The last of Juana's ties to Guatemala evaporated after her mother again became ill and finally died of cancer. Ms. García spent 1978 and 1979 in the United States with the help of her daughter, Gloria. (Still in Guatemala were two-year-old Sergio, Manuel, Aurelia, and Esperanza, left in the care of a neighbor.)

Juana set up a household with Gloria in the San Mateo area. She began working again, doing housecleaning to save money to bring the rest of the family north. Gloria was now 18 years old; she began to pull away from Juana's control and seek out a life of her own, eventually marrying and starting her own family in 1980. Juana began to worry more about her children back in Guatemala. She was receiving letters from her brothers and sisters reporting that the children were not living in clean conditions, that they were not well supervised, and that they had lice. Sergio had also injured his eye playing outside. Juana was told that he needed an operation. In spite of their estrangement, Juana wrote to Sebastián Sotelo, the father of the three children, and he brought them to stay with their aunt, Hortencia, Juana's oldest sister. In 1980, Juana decided that she had to move more quickly to bring her children north. She returned to Guatemala, had Sergio's eye taken care of, and put her house up for sale. By this time, her long-range intentions had changed. She could no longer afford to maintain a home in Guatemala. Therefore, she decided that the children would do better living in the United States. They could learn English, find jobs, and have a better future than they could in their own country. Back home, even if they studied hard, there was no future for them, no work. Besides, she added, the bombings, the killings, all of that meant that it was dangerous to walk in the streets. It was better for the family to move to the United States.

The Journey and Settling In

Ms. García applied for tourist visas for her children in 1980, but she soon found that she couldn't obtain them. She tried for student visas as well, but again she had no luck. It was starting to look as though she had no choice but to go overland. Selling her home took a long time, she said; there were a number of people who wanted to purchase it, but no one had the ready cash. After three months, Ms. García finally found a purchaser, so with the cash in hand from the sale of the house and the money from the furniture, Juana was able to accumulate enough money to get the family into the United States.

An acquaintance of Juana had a daughter whose boyfriend was American of Mexican descent. This daughter offered to help Juana bring her children across the U.S. border.

She charged us $350 per person. This was in 1981. We met her in Guatemala and we all traveled together until we got to the border. Then my sister [Marina] met us and took Aurelia and Sergio across the border herself. She used birth certificates of other children to get them across. My sister had her permanent residency green card by this time. That left Manuel, Esperanza, and me. The *señorita* and her boyfriend brought us to the ocean at six in the morning. It was high tide so we couldn't walk on the beach or cross the canal. We had to hide in the sand with pieces of driftwood all over us and wait for the tide to go down. About two in the afternoon, the tide was low enough for us to travel. We set off running. We had to run a long way, partly in the water, several miles at least. It took us about two hours. We were cold, wet, nervous, and feared being caught and sent back. I was particularly afraid for the children. For myself, it was all right. We didn't see anyone else running along the beach. We were the only ones—just me, Manuel, Esperanza, and the woman with her boyfriend. Marina met us at a pre-arranged spot, and we were all reunited.

When I asked Ms. García about how she felt the experience had been for her children, she said that she has heard many stories from other local Guatemalan families of difficult experiences that they have had, but that she herself felt good about how things worked out for her children.

When Juana first came to the United States she stayed with her sister. On later trips, she could always move in temporarily with her sister and daughter until she was on her feet with a live-in job or other kind of work. She got her job referrals from her sister and her daughter. Even the small house that the family is now renting in the San Mateo area was originally home for her sister Marina. When Marina moved out, Juana and her family took over the house. Juana is pleased with this small one-bedroom house they now occupy. One day during an interview, she showed me a new set of furniture that she had bought. She had bought it at a flea market sale, and she was especially proud to have gotten it as a set and at a good price. Aurelia and Esperanza are not as enamored of the home as is Juana. Aurelia, in particular, complains that her home in Guatemala was bigger. She says that there you could do whatever you want, put up pictures and so forth. Here the landlord doesn't want holes in his walls. Her mother counters by saying that back in Guatemala people out on the streets would break your windows and that there was nothing you could do about it. They were poor and couldn't get restitution. Little Manuel says he likes the United States better because he can ride his bike on the sidewalk.

Family members also disagree about the schools here in comparison with Guatemala. Esperanza feels that she is getting a better education here than in Guatemala. The students respect the teachers more, and she likes the classes. Aurelia and her brother say they don't like the teachers here. They say that the teachers yell too much. Ms. García started attending English classes herself, but she stopped going after a while because she was too tired after work and she had to travel to the lessons on the bus at night. Esperanza and Aurelia are in the eighth and seventh grades, respectively, and they are doing satisfactory work in general. However, both of them are having some trouble in English and in reading. One problem is that they never completed their formal language training in Spanish back in Guatemala. Thus, their capability in Spanish is limited, and it is difficult for them to translate the concepts into English when they have not learned them well in Spanish. They preferred talking to me in English during the interviews, and they tell me they think in English more than they do in Spanish. They are caught inbetween because they lack communication skills in both Spanish and English, and they are still working on the transition. In any case, language skill causes much anxiety in this family.

Both Aurelia and Esperanza compensate for their language deficits by being strong in math. They get A's in math and in physical education. They also do well in crafts and arts. Aurelia is quite put off by the curriculum on sex education that she is getting in her health class. She says that she doesn't like the subject and that social studies is boring, too. Aurelia and Esperanza do not socialize extensively with other Latino students. (They call them "Spanish.") Although Esperanza's best friend is Salvadoran, in general, they keep their distance from groups of Latinos. Aurelia and Esperanza do not speak Spanish at school except to help translate for a teacher or something like that. They tell me that they feel uncomfortable with the "Spanish" students because they talk in Spanish. They feel that the non-Spanish students will be insulted and think that the Spanish students are criticizing them. So they avoid being put in this uncomfortable position by avoiding the Spanish students. Esperanza also says that the Spanish students were unfriendly to her when she first arrived in the school. It seemed that they already had their friendship groups and that they were not open to newcomers. She says she felt bad when she was snubbed by the Spanish students and she could not communicate with the other students either. So she says that she had a very hard time during that first year in the United States.

Aurelia has ambitions to be a policewoman, or a computer programmer, or, as a last resort, to join the army. She thinks it would be "fun." Esperanza wants to be a doctor or a nurse. If she cannot afford the education, she would settle for an allied health profession. Esperanza met a woman who is a doctor in a hospital nearby their home, when she accompanied a friend with a broken finger to the hospital. Esperanza was quite impressed with this doctor, and now she returns periodically to visit the woman and to talk to her about being a doctor. Ms. García is somewhat discouraging about Esperanza's ambitions, saying she knows that the family cannot afford medical school.

Ms. García is sensitive to health problems in her family. She is aware that her children may have suffered from malnutrition while they lived in Guatemala under the care of a neighbor. Ms. García says that the neighbor spent all of the money that she sent for her children on the neighbor's own family, leaving very little for Ms. García's children. They had to eat tortillas cooked with onions all of the time, a diet lacking in variety and essential nutrients. Aurelia sees her health as somewhat better than that of her other brothers and sister. She says that in Guatemala she scrounged around to find all kinds of "junk" to eat. Also, she and her brother (the elder Manuel) raised a vegetable garden that added to the variety of available foodstuff. Juana says that the children were pale and thin when they first came to the United States. Now they eat better, they have new clothes, and their health is improved. Esperanza and Aurelia confirm that they are in better health here, but both of them tell me that they have trouble sleeping at night. Esperanza, in particular, says that worry keeps her awake and that sometimes she forgets to eat and consequently loses weight. She says that she is a very sensitive person, that she reacts strongly to what is going on around her.

Ms. García was in an automobile accident a year ago and has had pain in her back ever since. Although she was examined, x-rayed, and put on a physical therapy regimen, Ms. García says that the pain has never gone away and that she can do nothing to relieve it except take an occasional pain medication. She received this medication from the orthopedic doctor she has been seeing. Insurance from the drivers of both autos covers her medical expenses. No doubt her occupation as a house-cleaner exacerbates the injury, but Ms. García feels that there is nothing she can do. Sometimes she asks Esperanza to stay home from school and go to work with her to help out when she feels badly. She does this rarely, but Esperanza is worried about her mother's health and strength.

Juana has little respect for the county medical system. She brought her children for examinations after they arrived from Guatemala. They were physical exams needed for entering school. The doctor didn't do anything, she says. He just looked at them, asked them to stick out their tongues, and that was it. Marina told her about a neighborhood health clinic in San Francisco that was better. She took the children there and they gave them a complete examination. They only charged six dollars per person, too. Juana had to have a "D and C," or "cleansing of her womb," so she went to the county hospital herself. She paid them $50 on the spot, but afterwards she still kept getting annoying bills, thus confirming her bad opinion of the hospital.

Ms. García has worked as a housekeeper since her arrival in the United States. She has had no trouble finding jobs, but she has not always been pleased with her treatment at work. She told me one story of how she waited three hours outside in the cold for an employer to come home to let her in the house. She had just washed her hair, and she didn't have a sweater. The next day she caught the flu. This was a job she had as a live-in domestic when she was new in the country. The employer had forgotten his appointment with her, and when he finally appeared he was very unconcerned about the slip-up. Ms. García is quite upset about these and other slights and humiliations, saying that when people become rich they forget what it is like to be poor.

Ms. García's housework is the sole support for the family. Esperanza works with her on Saturdays. In this way Esperanza makes some money for herself as well. Half of her earnings go to her mother, and half she keeps. (Esperanza says that she is saving up for a car.) Ms. García began a small business this last Christmas, when she made up some fancy Christmas baskets with ornaments, candles, food, and other little items. She sold them to her employers, and then she and her sister went visiting Marina's friends and sold six more baskets. Ms. García says she enjoyed doing this but that the work takes time. She is tired and appears depressed; in any case, she is not sure she will have the energy to do it again.

Ms. García's low energy and depression means that she also does not have time or the will for friendships. She has never felt very close to any of her siblings, except for Marina. None of the family in Guatemala approved of her coming to the United States. She says that the only people she socializes with are Marina and her own married daughter Gloria. There have been tense relations even with Marina and Gloria over the last few years, although Juana declines to go into details. She asserts, though, that friends just bring trouble. "People like to visit just to criticize."

Some of Juana's withdrawal from a social life is related to some bad experiences she had with a local Pentecostal church. The García family has always been Catholic. But when Gloria came to the United States, she converted to an evangelical faith through her involvement with the local Pentecostal church. Juana followed her example, and she and the other children began attending as well. Juana was never convinced that it was what she wanted; however, the church actively recruited her. (She says she never did like all of that speaking in tongues, crying, and yelling. It didn't feel right to her.) Her son, Manuel, met another young man in the church who Juana says started putting a lot of bad ideas into his head:

He told Manuel that he was too dependent on his mother. Manuel started going with a Salvadoran girlfriend (who couldn't even speak Spanish properly) and staying out until four or five in the morning. I didn't stand for it. So he moved away from home and went to live with this young man. Now, this man had three sisters who also attended the church. They started inviting Esperanza to stay overnight. After a few visits, Esperanza began changing too. She would go out without asking permission. Another woman in the church told me, "Let her go." But I observed that this woman's own son does whatever he wants. I decided that was enough. I forbade Esperanza to go there. I stopped going to that church; I don't like how they take your children away from you.

The Adolescent and Family Culture

Ms. García has fought a lonely battle to get the family where it is today. All five of her children are now living in the United States, and she brought them up virtually on her own, with only the help of her sister, Marina. She has accomplished her major goal in life, it appears, and she has now lost her will and strength. She is a woman who has lived by her wits, and she has developed a strong measure of cynicism and worldly sensibility. The burden of raising a family of five alone without the support and backup of a husband or strong family of origin has taken its toll on her stability at times. Her children report that she sometimes "acts crazy" and gets in "bad moods."

Ideally, Juana sees herself as an individual with her own ideas, not following any particular cultural pathway. For example, she says that she is different from other Latinos in that she thinks that her daughters should be allowed to wear short skirts, makeup, and go out with their friends. She thinks that this freedom of the young is better than in Guatemala where the children are put down. She has also had enough of organized religion where they try to tell you what to do. Aurelia and

Esperanza, however, dress fashionably but conservatively. They do not wear makeup, and they do not see their mother as particularly liberal. They describe her as strict. Juana really keeps her daughters under a good deal of control in that she fears she will eventually lose her influence with them here in the United States. Esperanza already has found an American boyfriend at school, but she has not yet found the right moment to tell her mother about him.

The García family is an achievement-oriented family that wants to get ahead in the United States. They see the United States as the ticket to better jobs and a better life for the children. The family works to achieve these goals through a controlling and conforming ethos. However, in that the Latino values of respect for parent and teacher authority are opposed to the U.S. emphasis on freedom and openness, the family finds itself embroiled in constant conflict and division. This is reflected in the high family incongruence score of 23.3 and in the high Family Environment Scale scores in control, achievement, and conflict. The lowest scores in this family are in independence, cohesion, and recreation. Thus, the control is expressed erratically and rigidly, rather than through organized rules (see Figure 5).

The central theme in this family is one of assimilation. They have bought into the American dream with a vengeance. In terms of emotional and symbolic ties to Guatemala, the family is almost at a complete loss. I asked a number of questions relating to this theme in the interview process, and every time the family members would state that they have no ties, that they do not miss anything, and that they have no interest in ever returning. Juana did allow that she occasionally missed one or two of her sisters. And Aurelia was adamant that Christmas and other holidays were "boring" in the United States in comparison with the gay time to be had in Guatemala. "Here all you do is eat and open presents, sit and talk, and eat again. Back in Guatemala, you have fun!"

The García family members are avid followers of U.S. popular culture. They watch sitcoms and adventure shows on television; they eat spaghetti, hamburgers, and other simple U.S.-style meals (no soups or beans, as was their custom in Guatemala); and the teenage girls like to go to the shopping mall with their friends to shop for the latest fashions. The girls have no interest in the traditional *quinceñeros* for themselves when they turn 15, even though their cousins had it in Guatemala. They are particularly negative about Latino boys. Their mother tells them that there is a clear dichotomy between the Latino boys, who tend to mistreat girls, and American boys, or the "blue-eyes," who are more trustworthy. Esperanza and Aurelia think that she is probably right.

Along with the assimilation theme in this family is the corollary that one must "go it alone." Ms. García told me that it is better to lose your way alone than have someone lead you astray. Another time, she said that she thinks it is better to solve problems alone without anybody's help. She didn't want to give advice even to other immigrants because she says she doesn't want to be responsible for what might happen. This is an extremely individualistic stance, and it makes for a bewildering sadness, loneliness, lack of communication, and fear among the family members.

The emphasis on individualistic adaptation and change can be seen in the results of the FACES testing in that the family members seem frustrated with what they see as too-structured or rigid constraints. All would like to be more flexibly adapted or assimilated into the American dream (see Figure 6).

Aurelia is the only one who is holding back on a desire for change. She is still nostalgic for Christmas fun in Guatemala and she is not as achievement-oriented as either her mother or sister Esperanza. She, then, is the one who appears to be pulling the family back into some measure of balance.

The reporting of vivid and frequent dreaming by all family members also belies the family's single-minded path toward assimilation. These dreams illustrate the uncertainties, fears, and need for control and conflicts felt by all family members.

Aurelia reports frequent nightmares. In one, she is trying to hide as her mother chases her around the house. She also reports a recurrent dream in which a teacher kills another girl, puts her in a coffin, and then this dead girl tries to kill Aurelia. Aurelia's nightmares suggest she is preoccupied with fears of death and violence. These fears may derive from repressed experiences or simply too many television movies, but I suspect that much is symbolic of her dread of loss of identity, or her essence or soul, in her rapidly assimilating household.

Esperanza often dreams of carrying something heavy through a wide passageway. The trip is very long and she is frightened. She is trying to get somewhere but she isn't certain where. Just before my last visit, she told me of another dream. She was in a house owned by "some man." He was trying to kill everyone in the house. She either had to run away from him or stay in one place and "try to act like a dummy. Then he wouldn't kill you." One might interpret her first dream as one in which Esperanza carries the burden of the American dream. In her second dream, she finds herself in a dilemma that she has not yet resolved. She can either "act like a dummy" (follow other people's expectations?) and perhaps be safe, or she can make a run for it (take the initiative herself

FIGURE 5 - The García Family

Family Environment Scale

(FES)

Family Incongruence Score = 23.3

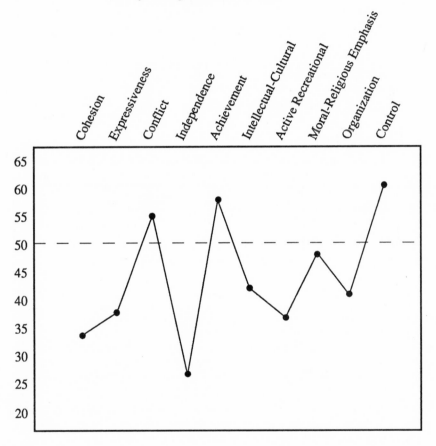

FIGURE 6 - The García Family
Family Adaptability and Cohesion Scale
(FACES)
Family Discrepancy Score = 11.2

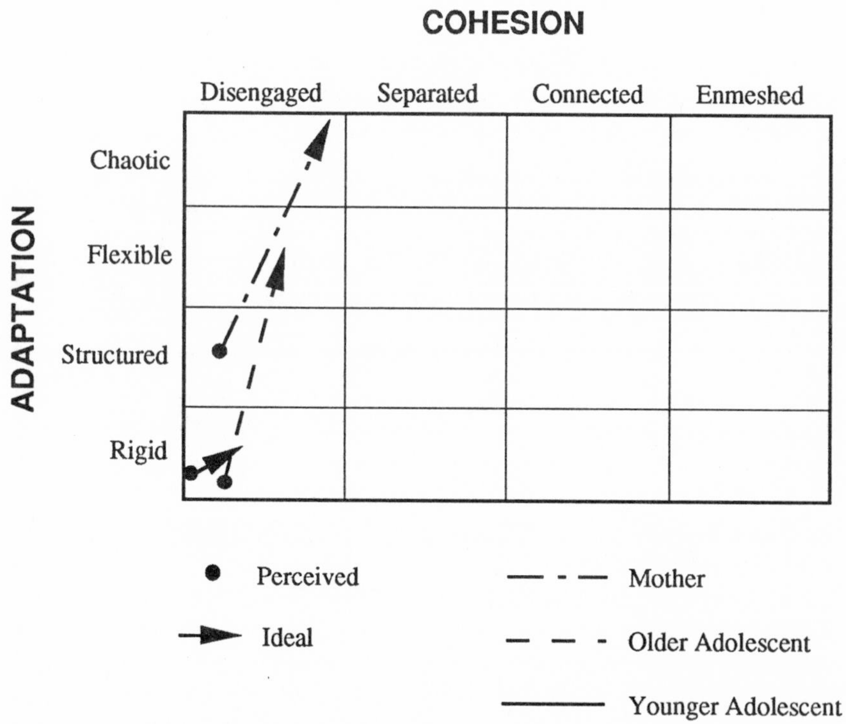

COHESION

ADAPTATION

	Disengaged	Separated	Connected	Enmeshed
Chaotic				
Flexible				
Structured				
Rigid				

●   Perceived   — · —   Mother

➤   Ideal   — — -   Older Adolescent

————   Younger Adolescent

and try to achieve what she wants for herself) and risk losing herself, her identity, a kind of death.

Juana, after all her protestations about Latino men and having no ties left to Guatemala, often dreams a romantic dream of Sebastián Sotelo, the father of Esperanza, Aurelia, and Sergio.   In this dream she re-integrates with a part of herself that she has openly rejected. She says that in her dream she is back in Guatemala, and Sebastián is making beautiful promises to her like he used to. In reality, she tells me, one of her sisters wrote to her that he actually came to the sister's home asking for Juana's address in the United States about a year ago. He said he wanted to come up and join her in the United States. When asked what she would do if he were to appear at her door, Juana laughed and said, "It would be better if that day God put me in the ground!"

Familismo, Nacionalismo, y Obligación: The Navarro Family

Origins

I came to know the Navarro family through a school counselor in a high school for immigrant students in San Francisco. He introduced me to Gordon, who was a bright and smiling, alert high school freshman.

Gordon lives with his mother and brother in the Mission district of San Francisco. At the time of the interviews they were living in a small rented room of a street-level flat on a busy street. Gordon was 13 years old; he turned 14 during the course of the interviews. Hugo is his nineteen-year-old brother. I interviewed both of them as adolescents for this study.

When I first came to the rented room to meet the family, Gordon was waiting out in front wearing overalls and a baseball cap. He looked much younger than when I met him in the high school. Hugo was very tall and slender. He was reserved and cautious in his contacts with me, rarely smiling. He glanced at me suspiciously from time to time, and he appeared to be strongly protective of his mother.

Ana Lucía Navarro is a handsome woman with dark hair and eyes. She is gracious and expressive, proud and worried. Other than Ms. Navarro's sister-in-law with whom the family has little contact, there are no relatives or extended family members in the vicinity. The family is a small three-member nuclear household; they are Catholic and attend mass regularly together, except for Hugo who is "not interested."

Ms. Navarro is one of seven children (Oswaldo Rubén, 50; Ana Lucía,

48; Carmen Alaíde, 46; Irma Clarisa, 36; Delfina Luisa, 34; Norma Susana, 30; and Emilio David, 24), all born and raised in a village near Cobán in the Department of Alta Verapaz.

As the oldest daughter, Ana Lucía was put to work early. She had to care for her four much younger brothers and sisters by her mother's second marriage. Although she went to school through the fourth grade and learned to read and write, her mother was explicit that she did not want Ana Lucía to learn a profession. She only wanted her to work. Therefore, Ana Lucía helped out working with her mother's bread-making business. She accompanied her mother when she went to market to sell her wares. Ana Lucía also had a number of other occupations such as domestic work, being a sales clerk in her grandmother's store, and picking coffee beans.

Ms. Navarro identifies herself socially as *Ladino*, but she shows evidence of strong personal loyalty and identification with the Kekchí Indian ethnicity. It is more than likely that she has at least some Kekchí ancestry.[7]

Ms. Navarro has never been married and her two sons are the offspring of two different fathers. Ana Lucía seems to be embarrassed about her "failures" with these two men. She did not become pregnant with Hugo, her first child, until she was 29 years old. At this time, she was still helping at home raising her younger brothers and sisters. Becoming pregnant by a man from neighboring Cobán seems to have been a convenient way for Ana Lucía to leave home. She says her mother became ill when she got pregnant, blaming Ana Lucía, and her mother has never been the same since then. When she was five months along in her pregnancy, she moved to Guatemala City and joined her older brother and next younger sister. They had trained to be nurses, and by now Oswaldo Rubén, her older brother, was an ambulance driver. Ana Lucía found work as a store clerk and as a domestic and settled into her new life in Guatemala City. After five years living in Guatemala City, she became pregnant again with Gordon. His father was a neighbor of hers, and he worked in a company that manufactured curaçao.

Ana Lucía never has allowed the fathers of either Hugo or Gordon to see their sons or to help support them even when they have expressed interest. She says she thinks it is not good because it "opens the door." Ana Lucía's mother was adamant about this. As Ana Lucía feels that both men were more interested in chasing skirts than in having a home and family, she has followed her mother's advice.

Ms. Navarro is now 48 years old. Her first twenty-nine years were spent living in a village near Cobán helping her mother. She tells me that she is very attached to the Alta Verapaz region where she spent most of her life, and that her family of origin is also very close knit. After all, she raised her younger brothers and sisters. Back home in the Alta Verapaz, she had to rise at three o'clock in the morning to begin to work. Her brother Oswaldo Rubén and next younger sister Carmen Alaíde despaired of making a life for themselves in this way, but Ana Lucia endured it. The next twelve years of her life were spent mainly in Guatemala City. During this time she brought her mother to the city to live. Her mother became close to her grandchildren, Ana Lucía's sons Hugo and Gordon.

The Decision to Move

Ms. Navarro told me of her decision to move to the United States in a very disjointed fashion. She began by telling me of her second of three trips to the United States. She often became confused about dates and related details of her third, more recent journey. Later, she amended her story to say that she had actually come to the United States three times instead of twice, as she had originally told me. Her story of her first brief sojourn in the United States was sketchy, and she frequently focused on certain events or pieces of events that had an emotional significance to her. In doing this she omitted important details that would lend a clearer understanding of the linear sequence and of the motivational context. In spite of my attempts to follow a semi-structured interviewing path in my questions, Ana Lucía often took our meetings as a time in which she could unburden herself of a number of her worries, anxieties, and painful memories in a cathartic manner.

Ana Lucía first began thinking of coming to the United States in 1969 when Gordon was born. Her sister Irma Clarisa had married a man whose mother lived in Washington, D.C. Ana Lucía wrote to her asking for help in coming to the United States. She wrote back saying that she would be happy to help her; they could share the rent in her apartment and she would help her find a job. She also sent her the plane fare, and Ana Lucía secured a tourist visa easily and flew to Washington, D.C. She left her children (Gordon was eleven months and Hugo was seven years old) in the care of Irma Clarisa. Unluckily, however, Ana Lucia's grandmother became very ill shortly after Ana Lucía left for the United States. As her condition was grave, Ana Lucía returned home by plane immediately.

Events occurred in 1976 that led Ms. Navarro to seek to return to the United States. The earthquake of that year flattened the little store that Ana Lucía was working in. After the main quake came a series of tremors that kept the area foundation weak. It was impossible to build a new store while the ground was still shaking. Meanwhile, there was no work, no income for the family. There was no work to be found elsewhere in the city either since the devastation was so widespread. One day three months after the earthquake, Ana Lucía was reading *La Prensa Libre*, Guatemala's primary newspaper when something caught her eye. It was an announcement of "excursions to the United States." Right then, she says, she decided that she was going.

Ana Lucía went to the "travel agency" that had advertised in the newspaper. She met the man who was in charge of the journey and told him that she wanted to go. She says that he smiled at her as though it were foolish for her, a woman, to go alone. But he told her that he had five years experience in running these trips and that it would cost her $350 to go to Los Angeles. She managed to raise the money she needed quickly from her family. Ana Lucía again left her two sons (by now ages eight and fourteen) in the care of her sister Irma Clarisa, and three days later she left. Her family was supportive of her trip at this time. Everyone wished her good luck.

The group that Ms. Navarro traveled with were from a variety of Central American countries. Most were from El Salvador. There were only six Guatemalans and only four women in the group, which numbered twenty-four in all.

Ana Lucía was apprehensive about the small number of women travelers and the fact that she knew no one in the group. She had good reason to be anxious about this trip. Unlike the first time she had come, this time Ana Lucía was traveling overland, *mojado*. (She says that it was impossible to get a tourist visa at that time. Too many people wanted to leave the country.)

The *coyote* took them via train, bus, car, and taxi. Only at the border to the United States did a problem occur. There, the *coyote* told the women that he wanted to bring them across one at a time. Of the four women in the group, one went with him. Ana Lucía and the other two women refused to travel in this way. They told him that they would rather be caught by the authorities than go in this way. The *coyote* then brought the three women to the guard at the checkpoint. He told the guard: "These three women are looking for fortune in the United States. They are honest women. They have suffered much tragedy at home, and their children are crying from hunger. Take pity on them, and let them pass." Ana Lucía says that the border guard acceded, saying that the women were obviously not drug dealers or troublemakers, so they could pass.

Some months later, Ana Lucía heard through other travelers on the journey that the woman who had gone over alone with the *coyote* was pregnant. She confessed that the *coyote* had threatened to abandon her in the mountains unless she submitted to him. Ms. Navarro did not tell me this story of the rape the first time she told me about her migration experiences. Only later, when I was reviewing some of the things she had told me and I asked her specifically about *coyotes* taking advantage of women, did she relate these subsequent events. As she spoke in a clipped and detached manner, I wondered if Ana Lucía herself had suffered any experiences of this kind and did not want to relate them due to either shame (*vergüenza*) or "psychic numbing."

On this second journey to the United States, Ana Lucía says she stayed for two years in San Francisco working as a domestic and taking care of elderly people in their homes. As time went by, she began to worry about her sons and about the bad news she was hearing about conditions in Guatemala. She decided to return and see for herself. When she arrived in 1978, she expected there to be a tidy sum of money in her bank account. She had been sending regular remittances to her sister Irma for the care of her sons. But to her dismay there was only $48 left in her account, and her sons seemed ill-clothed and ill-cared for. She confronted her sister, who responded that expenses were high that the boys had wanted this and that, and that medical expenses for when they were ill had eaten up the rest of the savings. Ana Lucía was quite upset at this discovery. Her plan had been to earn enough money in the United States so that her children could buy clothing and attend school in Guatemala, but this plan was not working out. She felt that she could not count on her family to care for her sons adequately. "They did their best."

Ana Lucía started thinking of bringing the boys to the United States. Other compelling reasons began to increase her resolution to do this. In 1978, Guatemalan president Lucas García had unleashed the death squads. Ana Lucía says, "I couldn't go downtown. If you left your home, you would be lucky if you got back." Incidents of assassination, kidnapping, torture, and terrorism were happening daily. "Not frequently," Ms. Navarro corrected me, "continually." Hugo informed his mother that his girlfriend had been kidnapped and that his friend had been shot. Ms. Navarro relates, "We didn't know who was doing this. One day, my sons were in a barber shop getting a haircut. Two men with masks entered the shop, grabbed a man seated there, and dragged him away with them. Another day, they got up in the morning to see a truck parked on the street near their home with the truck driver murdered inside."

At the same time, the countryside of Alta Verapaz was also the scene of a number of massacres, assassinations, kidnappings, and terrorist activities. It was not safe to return there, either, although that is where

Ana Lucía thought to go, since most of her family was still there or had returned when things turned so ugly in Guatemala City.

The last straw for Ana Lucía was when her older brother, Oswaldo Rubén, was kidnapped. Ana Lucía had no theory as to why he was singled out.

Perhaps he saw something. He was an ambulance driver. But my sister called me one day and told me that he had disappeared. We made up some lies for my mother so she wouldn't worry, and I went to my sister in Alta Verapaz. We heard he was in a hospital in Salamá. He had been captured after he left work. Some men had grabbed him, tied him up, tortured him, and beaten him senseless. They had burned his feet with cigarettes. He had three broken ribs. He lost one eye from what they did to him. They left him for dead in a ravine, but he wasn't dead. He climbed up the hill and escaped. No one wanted to help him; everyone was too frightened. But somehow he made it to this hospital in Salamá. When we found out where he was, we came and got him out of the hospital at once. If the men had found out where he was, they would have come back to the hospital and killed him right there.

We hid him and took him to Guatemala City to the hospital there. My sister-in-law, my brother's wife, was the one who was most affected by this. She began screaming and crying. She got really bad and had to see a doctor herself. She finally ended up coming with me to the United States when I came this last time. She needed to make some money to pay for all the medical expenses for my brother.

Two months after Ana Lucía's brother was kidnapped and tortured, Ana Lucía, her two sons, and Oswaldo Rubén's wife left for the United States. Ana Lucía felt that they had to get away from the horror. The decision was hers, although family considerations (medical expenses for her brother, a future for her sons) played a paramount role as well. Gordon did not want to come, but Hugo says that he did want to make the trip. He was evasive as to why, saying he wanted to "find out about the United States for himself." He did not mention to me anything about a girlfriend or male friend either kidnapped or shot, or anything else of that nature.

The Journey and Settling In

This last journey to the United States in 1981 was the third for Ana Lucía but the first for her sister-in-law and for her sons. Ms. Navarro is quite bitter about the experience, saying that it was the most difficult thing she has ever had to endure. She says that for the amount of money she spent on coming to San Francisco *mojado* as they did, all four of them could have flown back and forth to Guatemala City "in pure comfort." Of course, this would have been impossible because they had no access to tourist visas or legal amenities of any kind. Instead, the entire family pooled whatever resources they could muster in order to amass the $4,000 needed to pay the *coyote* for the trip. The *coyote* promised that they would not have to climb mountains, that legal documents would be purchased for the travelers, and that the trip would be all-expenses-paid.

The day they were to leave, the group met in the *coyote's* home.

He leveled with us at this time. He told us that we should not bring any luggage, just the clothes on our backs. He said we would travel as tourists only through Mexico. Going into the United States, we would have to climb mountains, walk on foot, and so on. If we were caught by immigration authorities, we would be sent back to Guatemala. He then asked if anyone wanted to back out. He informed us that if anyone changed their minds at this point they would forfeit $300 of the $1,000 they had already paid. We felt we had no choice; we had to continue.

We set out for Mexico. The deception continued at the Guatemala-Mexico border when we were told to pay for the hotel and meals. The *coyote* left us at the border, giving us only directions as to how to proceed. The next day, we caught a train for Guadalajara. There we had to wait for three days until a bus came that we could take to Nogales at the U.S. frontier. We had to pay our own expenses in Guadalajara, and, in addition, they forced us to pay for useless identification papers for each of us saying that we were Mexican and from Guadalajara. I had only brought $200 extra cash with me.

At six o'clock in the morning, a man met us at the Tijuana border as we had been told. He told us to wait in line and when people go to the right, you go to the left. We waited in the bathroom until we got a signal. Then we got in line. We had to hold the catch on the gate so that the buzzer wouldn't make a sound. Then we ran to the bus station in San Ysidro and caught the bus to San Diego. There were two cars waiting for us at the bus terminal. Two of us got in one car, two got in the other. They took us to a house in San Diego. The woman there was going to charge us two dollars per person for room and board, but by this time I had no more money. That night we slept on the floor in the same clothes that we had worn when we left Guatemala fifteen days earlier.

In the morning, my sister-in-law and I cleaned up the house for the woman who had gone to work. When she returned, she was pleased, so she gave us food and allowed Gordon to sleep in the same bed with her son. The next morning it was the turn of another woman traveler to go to Los Angeles. However, she balked when she was put in the trunk of the car for the trip. Since she refused to travel that way, we agreed to take her place. All four of us got into the trunk. They had some kind of air vent so that we could breathe. Nevertheless we were frightened. My sister-in-law brought some pills for nerves with her, so we took these pills when we got into the trunk. Except for Hugo and Gordon; they weren't scared at all. We stayed like that for three and a half hours until we got to Los Angeles. When they opened the trunk and hustled us out of there, we all had such headaches!

In Los Angeles we called an uncle of my sister-in-law. We had a little scare because at first this uncle didn't remember her; he hadn't seen her in many years. But he finally did, and then he took us in. This uncle drove us to San Francisco the next day to the home of a friend of mine who is Mexican.

Ana Lucía says she moved around various times before she found the room that she and her sons were living in at the time of my interviews. For the first three months she and her sons stayed with Mexican friends in Alamo, a town some distance from San Francisco. Ms. Navarro then took a live-in job caring for a sick and demented woman in Pacifica who needed around-the-clock care—feeding, bathing, medication, and so on. She left her sons in the care of a relative of her friend in Alamo who lived in Union City. The friend promised to bring her sons to visit her on weekends. However, after a couple of months, Hugo and Gordon complained that they did not like Union City, that there were too many Mexicans drinking and fighting, and that it was not a comfortable place for them to stay. So Ms. Navarro took out an advertisement on the Spanish language radio station in San Francisco offering to pay $350 per month to a family who would take care of her sons. She found a woman who lived in Daly City who promised to provide meals and a room for the boys, so she left them there.

Ms. Navarro was beginning to feel very pressured and emotionally upset and drained. Working to care for the woman was very difficult; the woman was argumentative and would hit her and kick her when she tried to bathe her and feed her. She was generally abusive and Ana Lucía did not believe in returning this kind of treatment, so she just put up with it. The woman was from Costa Rica, but her daughter, Ms. Navarro's employer, told her that she herself didn't like Latinos. Ana Lucía says she was very hurt and upset working for her because the daughter did not treat her well. The daughter left her alone with the mother all of the time and practically never talked to her. This meant that Ana Lucía was completely isolated from any social contact except for the senile mother.

Ms. Navarro began to feel worse and worse. She was getting bad headaches all of the time and she felt like she was trapped. Whenever she saw or talked to her sons, she felt better; but this was only twice a month when she was free to leave. Finally, she called a psychologist whom she heard about on the Spanish language radio station. The Latino psychologist came out to visit her three times in the home where she was working. He charged her $20 per visit, and she says that he did her a lot of good. He told her that she was under too much strain and that she could not take on so many problems. He told her that the letters she was receiving from home were causing her much grief, that she should give him any letters she received and that he would read them and tell her if there was any good news in them. If there wasn't, he would keep the letters and not tell her what was in them. She says he also gave her some sleeping medication, but only a few pills, because he didn't want her to become dependent on them. The doctor also advised her to leave her job and not seek any more live-in work. He said that she needed to be with her sons and to find other work where she would have her own home to go to after work.

At this point, Ms. Navarro left the job after enduring it for ten months. Her employer put a lot of pressure on her to stay, saying that her mother was now accustomed to Ana Lucía and that they could not get along without her. But, armed with the doctor's advice, Ms. Navarro was adamant. She went to see her sons in Daly City and found that things were not as they should be. The sons were being fed just rice and beans, and they had been forced to sleep on the floor. They had not complained this time; perhaps they had been too concerned about their mother. (They had already complained once about Union City, and they had then moved to Daly City. No doubt they felt that Ms. Navarro could not have tolerated any more bad news from them.) This time, however, Ms. Navarro took more time in picking the next room and board locale for her sons. She found a home in the Mission district of San Francisco, and she interviewed the woman of the house carefully before she agreed to place her sons there. Ana Lucía and her sons liked this woman and her family, her sons were treated well, and the families became friends. But a number of newly arrived Salvadoran friends and relatives began to crowd the home. So Hugo and Gordon moved back in with their mother in the one room she was renting nearby.

During the time I was interviewing the Navarro family, this rented room was the scene of my visits. The Navarro family rented the room from another family who took in boarders. Ms. Navarro did not like this arrangement; she was uncomfortable with the landlady, whom she felt was unfriendly and inhospitable. She didn't feel she could relax and use the facilities (kitchen, bathroom, telephone, common hallway, etc.) Since the time of the interviews, Ms. Navarro has called me twice on the telephone to inform me that she has moved. Each time there seems to be a problem, but the main one is the expense of housing in the area for a single mother with teenage sons.

Ms. Navarro now works cleaning various houses five days a week. She gets $25 a day, and she travels as far as Sausalito and Burlingame.

She found her first jobs through a woman she met on the bus. Since then, some of her employers have given her other referrals. She is happy with her working conditions now, saying that here in the United States she is generally treated better by her employers. In Guatemala, they think nothing of having you work from five in the morning until two the next morning. Here, sometimes, her employers will even work along with her, or they will say to her that she should leave some of the work for another day.

Ms. Navarro's main concern regarding work has to do with her son Hugo. Hugo was not working during the time I was interviewing the family. It appears that her worry was as much about the trouble he might get into "on the streets" as with the lack of family income. Hugo did work for a short time in a upholstery factory, but he left the job because there were threats of immigration raids and the bosses were making him work much harder than the other workers who were family and friends of the bosses. When I interviewed the family, Ana Lucía's concern was that Hugo would not be able to find work and that he would become discouraged and lose interest in even trying to look. She feared he would get mixed up in some kind of trouble on the street. Later, when she called me after the interviews were complete, she was very relieved to inform me that Hugo had found work, that he was working regularly doing construction.

School is a topic of much interest to the entire family. It may be that Ms. Navarro's mother's injunction that she should not get an education has had a reverse effect on the family. All three members of the family attend school. Ms. Navarro and Hugo study at night in adult school English classes. They go four nights a week. Gordon is a scholarship student who has been singled out by his teachers and counselors as having great potential. His mother is quite proud of his scholastic achievements, which include a number of certificates and prizes for attendance and good citizenship, and a scholarship to go to a backpacking camp in Yosemite through the Police Athletic League. He gets excellent grades, and his mother says the schoolwork is easy for him since school in the United States is so much easier than it is in Guatemala.

Gordon has already formulated career plans. His hero is a famous British agronomist whom he learned about in school. Gordon would like to be an "expert agronomist" himself some day and return to Guatemala as a professional. Hugo, his older brother, has more modest goals. He wants to learn enough English so that he can find work more easily. Someday, he would like to own his own grocery store—like his hero, his uncle Rony back in Guatemala. But he does not want to return to

Guatemala, he says. He feels he has already made a choice, that he had to make a clean break, not to look back or go back, for it would be too sad.

Ana Lucía and Hugo are preoccupied with similar problems in adapting to life in the United States. Ana Lucía is still quite worried about conditions at home for her family. She feels guilty for being here while many of her relatives have reported difficulties in Guatemala. A cousin of hers was shot and injured in a terrorist attack; his house was also burned to the ground. Her youngest sister, with whom she is the closest, attempted to come to the United States and was caught by the authorities and deported back to Guatemala. (What Ana Lucía heard was that another traveler in her sister's group—a male—told her that he would turn her in to the immigration police if she didn't sleep with him.) Finally, Ana Lucía has received letters recently from family members stating that her mother is ill with gastritis and is quite weak. The family is pressuring Ana Lucía to come home and take care of her. None of them approved of her bringing her sons to the United States in the first place. She feels she is fighting their disapproval all of the time.

Such news is distressing in that Ana Lucía is not really happy in the United States anyway. She is here only "out of necessity." Here in the United States she can make a decent income, whereas back home she could not. Ms. Navarro obviously misses her family and country intensely; in contrast to Guatemala, she feels people in the United States are not friendly. No one talks to her at church, and she sees that there are too many bad influences for young people to cope with here—for example, the *cholo* style of which she does not approve. She feels that in the United States parents do not keep their language and customs in the family. The children lose the ability to speak Spanish, and they lose respect for their parents. Some day she would like to go home.

Hugo is also unhappy here and distrustful of people. He and his brother had a difficult introduction to the United States, what with the difficult journey into the country as well as mistreatment since he has arrived. As is his style, he is reticent to go into detail about his difficulties, but they have evidently made him a suspicious and angry young man. He says that he is not interested in making friends, that friends only bring trouble, and that they are kind at first, but later on they show their true colors. He misses his group of friends back in Guatemala, and since he has been here he has made only one friend, another young Guatemalan man about the same age. Hugo is also resentful about what he sees as undue police harassment of youth on the streets. He says he has never had this kind of trouble himself, but he sees it a lot. Before he acquired the construction job he now holds, Hugo spent a lot of time at his Guatemalan friend's home "listening to the music that the *cholos* like." It is intriguing that Hugo professes to have no interest in the opposite sex. "*¿Para qué?*" (for what purpose?) he asked me. Although his mother told me that his girlfriend had been kidnapped and that another friend of his had been shot in Guatemala, he himself did not confirm this story. In fact, he denied having a girlfriend back in Guatemala. It seems that reunification with loved ones at home is either impossible or too much to hope for, so Hugo refuses to hope. As he put it, "It would be too sad." Likewise, Hugo avoids projecting his wishes too much into the future. The dream of one day owning his own store is as far as he will go.

Gordon, age 13 going on 14, is the family member with a future. He is the ideal student, and he has adapted to the U.S. school system so well that he has captured the attention of the teachers. Gordon has made a number of friends in school; he socializes easily, and his English is good. (He is not yet interested in girls, he says.) On one visit, he proudly showed me a large flag of Guatemala and the Guatemalan national anthem that he had drawn for a class assignment. So far, Gordon has managed to cope well outwardly with his competing loyalties—his teachers and his academic future in the United States versus his mother and Guatemala. However, his tense demeanor, inability to relax, and somatic complaints give clues of his internal struggle

The Adolescent and Family Culture

The central themes of the Navarro family are those of familism, nationalism, and obligation (*familismo, nacionalismo, y obligación*)—the ideology and the reality. The Family Environment Scale shows that the family scores highest in moral-religious orientation and family organization. Their lowest scores are in recreation, intellectual-cultural orientation, and conflict (see Figure 7). The family values reflected by the scores are sense of familial duty to elders, adherence to religious values, and loyalty to their country and region that is felt most keenly since they are away from familiar surroundings. Family members are strong nationalists. All show great pride in their country, and in some way they seem to have integrated both the Indian and *Ladino* identities in themselves. When she came to the United States, Ms. Navarro brought her *traje típico* (typical, or Kekchí dress) as well as a traditional silver chain necklace that comes from her region, Alta Verapaz. It took some special pains to accomplish this since her journey was so difficult. As in Guatemala, Ms. Navarro wears her *traje* on certain religious holy days such as the Day of the Virgin of Guadalupe. On numerous occasions, family members indicated their pride in Guatemalan customs and traditions. Once Ms. Navarro reprimanded me for not teaching my children adequate Spanish and for not being familiar with some of the national holidays and traditions. Ms. Navarro extended her partiality to her region and the Kekchí language with which she was raised. Her sons can also speak some Kekchí. At the same time, Ms. Navarro also is taking on some practical adaptations of life in the United States. She can be seen wearing blue jeans, and she is studying English.

The ideology of familism and obligation derives from the strong attachment that all family members have to the rules and organization of the extended family system. This bonding is partly an extension of the Guatemalan norm, but it takes on a covert and conflicted dimension in this particular family. Ana Lucía has been the individual in her family of origin who was designated to care for her mother. She is aware that her mother chose her for this task, and ever since her siblings and other relatives have reinforced this position for her. The reality is that Ana Lucía has tried numerous times to escape what was becoming a somewhat oppressive role. She had two children, but her mother did not approve of their fathers. She has come to the United States three times to support her family. The first two times she was called home by family obligations. The first time was because her grandmother was ill. The second time was because conditions in Guatemala were worsening and she was concerned about her sons and the rest of the family. Now she continues to receive letters from home reminding her of her mother's frail health and essentially asking her to return. She "acted out" this conflict by taking on a live-in job that was extremely difficult, the around-the-clock nursing of an elderly senile woman. Symbolically, it seemed Ana Lucía was caring for her mother in this position, and she was also taking on the role of nurse (professionally) that her brother and sisters had encouraged her to assume for their own mother. When the job proved to be impossible, she brought in a psychologist who gave her the courage to leave and strike out on her own. Thus, Ana Lucía has been able to resist the pull of family obligation so far.

In relation to her sons, Ms. Navarro would like to extricate herself from the strong duty she feels even to them. She seems to be fighting an adolescent battle for more independence for herself at the age of 48. This can be seen in the FACES test, where she indicates a desire for less family cohesion and more disengagement (see Figure 8). At the same time, Ana Lucía wants to pull in the reins and maintain tighter rules for her sons' behavior. She is mainly concerned about Hugo. Her FACES scoring shows a desire to move from a flexible adaptation to a more structured one.

Ms. Navarro has brought her children to the United States partly to extricate them from what she sees as a hopeless and dangerous situation for them, and partly because she needs them to take care of her. Both of her sons are struggling with their own adolescent needs in addition to the pressure for family reorganization and responsibility. They have responded in very different ways.

Hugo's dignity as the oldest male of the family (the symbolic father) was assaulted when he was mistreated on the journey and he was unable to defend the family from the injustices and privations they endured. This continued in Daly City when he and his brother were fed only rice and beans and they had to sleep on the floor. He reports a number of other experiences in which he has been humiliated—in working, and in watching the police rousting Latino street youth like himself. In addition, Hugo has been traumatized by the violent events in Guatemala. He does not want to talk about them or to face them. It would be "too sad." At age 19, he feels disengaged from the family and stuck in a slightly too rigid role, as indicated by the FACES scoring. His way of taking care of his mother, then, is to try to find work, to study English, and to avoid involvements with other youth who could tempt him to lose control in drinking and in other vices. He sees girls as just another temptation or a vice. A girlfriend would also raise conflicts for him vis-à-vis his loyalty to his mother. It is interesting that in the FACES scoring Hugo and his brother Gordon both desire more family connection, in contrast to their mother's desire to disengage.

Gordon's role in the family is quite different. The FACES test indicates that he feels much more strongly connected to the family than either his mother or Hugo. He wants even more connection and somewhat tighter and more secure family organization. When I met him at his home for the initial interview, at first I did not recognize him. He had appeared completely different when I first met him at his high school. There he had taken on the demeanor of a young high school student, alert and assertive. At his home, however, he looked years younger, sitting on the bed quietly with his baseball cap and overalls; he looked to be not much older than 10 years. Gordon also has two names. Outside the family, he is known by his given name, Gordon, a scholarly Anglo name. At home, though, he goes by Azzarro. It is a pet name, the name of a perfume. Azzarro-Gordon seems to cope well with these two identities. At times, though, the gap between the two identities—and the ideology of familism, nationalism, and obligation and the reality of his precarious, insecure existence—leads him to panic. He was disturbed, for example, by a recent dream. In it he was standing at the top of a cliff with a big crowd of people watching him. All he could think of was to

FIGURE 7 - The Navarro Family

Family Environment Scale
(FES)
Family Incongruence Score = 15.3

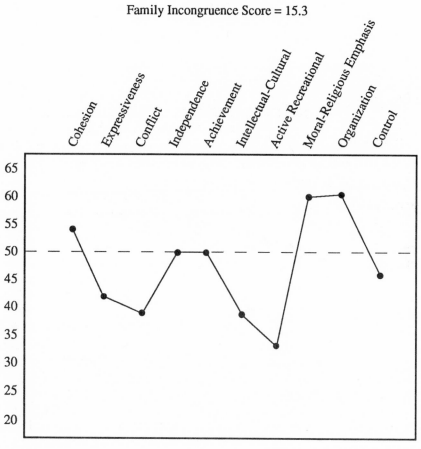

FIGURE 8 - The Navarro Family

Family Adaptability and Cohesion Scale
(FACES)

Family Discrepancy Score = 6.5

COHESION

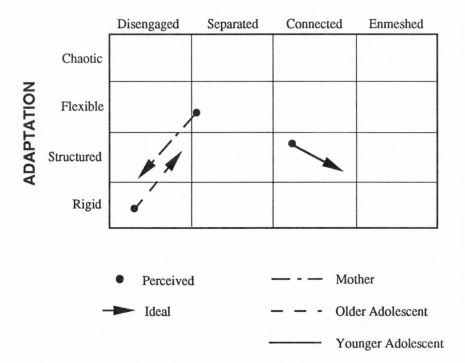

jump off. Then, he said, there would be no more problems. This dream is apparently a suicide dream. It would seem that Azzarro-Gordon is struggling to keep such desperate impulses under control.

Solidaridad, Disciplina, y Progreso: The Castillo Family

Origins

I met the Castillo family through a bilingual high school teacher in a small San Francisco high school that has a number of Latino students. He introduced me to Mario, who, at age 15, was a high school freshman. The teacher who referred this family was impressed with the parents' concern and involvement with their children's education. They had spoken to the counselor about entering their younger son in the school, and they had attended school functions with their son as well. Mario was a good-looking, friendly, relaxed student, short and athletic-looking. The teacher told me that he was a model student.

In spite of scheduling difficulties, both Mr. and Mrs. Castillo were jointly involved in planning for the interviews; they seemed to work very closely together. Mr. Julio Castillo is 38 years old and of medium height; he wears work clothes that are streaked with dirt. He has dark hair and eyes and his features are Indian. He has a quiet sense of security and dignity. Mrs. Yolanda Castillo is also 38 years old, of medium height and build, with dark hair and eyes. She is polite and reserved, soft-spoken and hospitable. She seems to be in a strong position of leadership in the family in that she only needs to scan the room briefly with her eyes for the rest of the family to respond to her. The family is Catholic and of working-class background.

Julio Castillo was born in Retalhuleu, a southwestern coastal department of Guatemala, but his family moved to Guatemala City when he was only five months old. This happened because his mother was marrying her fourth husband, Julio's stepfather. Most of Mr. Castillo's relatives have been either in the army or police, or they have been musicians. A number of them have been military musicians. Julio was raised by this stepfather, he said. He taught him to play the marimba in a band when he was eight years old. In the daytime he went to school up to the sixth grade. In the afternoons and evenings, he played in the band. The band played at private parties and for holidays and celebrations. Julio met Yolanda when he was 16 years old. He was a friend of Yolanda's brother, Leonel. Leonel brought him to the home, and he and Yolanda became sweethearts.

Yolanda is the fifth of nine siblings in a family from Guatemala City. She said that her family was very poor, so when she was young she had to work in coffee plantations. She managed to complete the sixth grade by the time she was 15 years old. At that time she began working in a factory where coffee beans were sorted. The good beans were set aside to be exported to foreign countries and the bad beans were for local consumption. Yolanda appears to have taken in this political lesson at that time. She made a number of comments of this type throughout the interviews.

Yolanda and Julio were married when they were both 20 years old. Julio continued to work as a musician as well as taking on a number of other occupations in the building trades. During the early years of their marriage, Yolanda did not work; she dedicated herself to raising her family. They began their family in 1968 when Mario was born. Next came Rodolfo, Roxanda, Adán, Lourdes, and Ernst. All of them were born in Guatemala. They all entered the United States in 1980. For the purposes of this study, I have interviewed the three eldest children as the adolescents of the family. They are Mario, now 15; Rodolfo, now 14; and Roxanda, now 12. Adán is 10; Lourdes is 9; and Ernst is 6.

The Decision to Move

Mrs. Castillo told her story in a straightforward manner, in a low voice, and without elaboration. She said she never had any intention to come to the United States. She said her sisters and her *comadre*[8] encouraged her to do so. One day her *comadre* told her that she was going to the United States; she wanted Yolanda to come with her. Yolanda already had three sisters who were living in San Francisco, so it seemed like a good time to join them. Yolanda said that life in Guatemala at that time was difficult; it was harder and harder to make a living. She and Julio already had five children and they wanted to buy a little house. They could not hope to earn enough money to do this in Guatemala. Yolanda hoped that she could accumulate enough cash in the United States so the family would be able to afford a down payment on a house in Guatemala. In 1975, two weeks after her *comadre's* request, Yolanda and her *comadre* were on their way to San Francisco. Here Yolanda readily found work cleaning houses through ads in local newspapers.

The earthquake of 1976 brought Mrs. Castillo back home to Guatemala earlier than planned. In the next two years she helped in reconstruction efforts and she and Julio had their last child, Ernst. Mrs. Castillo went back and forth to the United States alone one more time in 1978-1979 with the help of her younger sister who had married a U.S. citizen; this last time she decided that it was bad for the family to be separated. Julio's mother was not strict enough with the children, so she spoke to Julio about the entire family coming to the United States together.

Julio had a slightly different notion. He spoke to his employer, who suggested that he develop a new career for himself as a topographer with the appropriate training in the United States. Julio traveled overland alone and entered the United States with a letter of introduction to an individual who he hoped would help him get started in this new career. His intent was eventually to return to Guatemala in this profession and to purchase a house.

Mrs. Castillo, on the other hand, was mainly concerned with keeping the family intact. She did not want to wait for the day when Julio would return and they could buy a house. Nor did she put a lot of stock in either Guatemala or the United States being intrinsically better places to live. (Mrs. Castillo is more of a cynic and realist than Mr. Castillo with regard to the wider community or national loyalty. She cares mostly for what is best for her family—herself, husband, and children.) In coming to the United States, though, Yolanda was reunited with three of her own sisters and separated from her parents and five other siblings. The reunification and separation have been both happy and painful for Yolanda. The two members of her original family that were most important in her life were her father and next older sister. When Yolanda was leaving Guatemala for the last time, this sister was living in San Francisco and encouraging her to come north. At the same time, her father was ill in the hospital in Guatemala. Although he knew that she was going to leave, he didn't know exactly when. As Yolanda didn't want to upset him, she never said goodbye to him. She just left one day with the children. During my interviews, Mrs. Castillo cried when she related this story. "My father loved me very much," she said. "We were always close. He never criticized me and we never fought." Her father died some months after Yolanda left Guatemala. To this day, she burns a candle in the apartment next to a picture of her father.

Mr. and Mrs. Castillo were very circumspect about what they told me of their motivations to come to the United States; they tended to downplay personal and political problems. Mrs. Castillo spoke in a low voice while the tape recorder was on, and they both gave brief responses to questions. They emphasized the economic reasons for the move and de-emphasized the impact of the war and of familial and personal problems. For example, later on in the interviews, they told me that Julio was drinking heavily in 1975 and that he had been in "an accident" in which some men jumped him and beat him up. But neither Julio nor Yolanda (in her husband's presence) acknowledged that the drinking had become a serious problem, even though Julio admitted that he ceased drinking altogether for over a year around that time.

All in all, the Castillo family members tended to be positive and future-oriented and to minimize the difficulties of the past (with the exception of Yolanda's father's death). In all of the interviews, both Mrs. and Mrs. Castillo were present. It was never possible for me to speak to either of them individually. When I interviewed the three adolescent children, they all stayed together as well, and they resisted being interviewed alone. Their parents also came in and out of the room while I talked to them, so that it was never possible for me to get them to give me candid opinions or private information on an individual basis. They seemed to look to each other a great deal for support, and as such they gave a very unified picture on most questions.

Mrs. Castillo has a number of relatives here; three of her sisters and her one brother are all living in the San Francisco Mission district. They see a lot of each other. Through Yolanda's sister, the family is already working with a lawyer to secure U.S. residency for all of them. But Yolanda avoids taking sole responsibility for bringing the family to the United States. Instead, she sensitively defers to Julio, who has no family here. Mr. Castillo's career plans in the United States were somewhat farfetched and, as it turned out, unattainable. Nonetheless, he has settled comfortably into the (ostensible) decision-maker role. He states that he would like to return to Guatemala "in a few years, after my children get their education." When pressed to be more specific, Mr. Castillo varies in his answer from five years to eighteen years on different occasions. Generally, in answering questions that I asked, Julio gave me general concepts in reply. When it came to details, Yolanda filled them in, sometimes correcting him on specifics. This couple is a decision-making team with Julio as the philosophical leader and Yolanda as the indispensable woman behind the man—and, probably, the true leader in the family.

Yolanda and Julio were clearly at odds about the political realities of Guatemala. Julio (who comes from a military family, but also a family of musicians) was supportive of Ríos Montt, the Guatemalan president during the time of my interviews. He felt that there were problems with corruption and unemployment, but that Ríos Montt was trying to straighten things out. He stated that it was often an unpopular task to root out corruption and that is why Ríos Montt has received such bad reception among some circles in Guatemala. He never indicated how the military members of his own family stood politically. On the other hand, Yolanda had no use for any politicians. She felt that they are all crooks and that it does not matter who is the president of the country. Any president would automatically take from and hurt the people of the country while supporting what he could get for himself in concert with foreign elites. In contrast to Julio, who said he thought conditions in Guatemala "have improved," Yolanda was sure that they had not and that the people being murdered by death squads are not just *guerilleros* but innocents for whom there is no justice or rule of law. She also had no use for Mejía Victores when he deposed Ríos Montt. She said he has kept the 10 percent surtax that was instituted by Ríos Montt and thus the government continues to rob the people. It was significant that when I asked Mr. and Mrs. Castillo how they dealt with their differences, they told me that they never discussed politics. They said that whenever the subject arises, they always bring the conversation back to family needs and concerns. This way they can focus on how the children are doing and how they can do better. "This is a topic on which we can always agree, so we prefer to discuss our children. Politics is an area in which no one is going to change their mind, so why discuss it?"

This family style of decision making is relevant to how the family decided to come to the United States. Mr. and Mrs. Castillo have found that they can make decisions with more tranquility and unaninimity when they focus on family needs such as buying a home and seeing that their children are well brought up and educated.

The fact that they entered the United States in 1980, a year in which there was a great deal of violence and terrorism in Guatemala City, was passed over lightly by Mr. and Mrs. Castillo. It is possible and even likely that Julio's military family was affected in some way by the growing war in Guatemala. But Julio tended to emphasize the musician and artist in himself. This was typical of his general approach to highly charged subjects related to conflict and violence. For example, he was "not really interested" in who murdered his father when Julio was a baby. (It is notable that his father was a military man who was murdered in 1945 shortly after Úbico left power and Arévalo came in with a new social order.) In this way, Julio seems to protect himself from knowledge that might prove to be dangerous to him and to his family.

The Castillo children ranged from 3 to 11 years at the time of their journey to the United States in 1980. They were not consulted about the trip. The two older boys, Mario and Rodolfo, then 10 and 11, did not want to come. Eight-year-old Roxanda (now 12) had a more adventurous spirit. She said that she wanted to come. Yolanda said that one factor that convinced her they needed to come at this time was the age of the children. She stated that because they were young, she could tell them what to do and expect no problems. She feared that if they had been much older they would have had loose tongues, thus making it more difficult to cross the border.

The Journey and Settling In

Mr. Castillo came to the United States "with friends" in 1979. Since he had acquaintances and his sisters-in-law living in San Francisco, he had a relatively uncomplicated border crossing, albeit undocumented. He managed to find work through his friends and settle into a living situation that would accommodate his family. The following year, Mrs. Castillo took out a loan to pay for the transportation and hotel expenses for herself and all of her children. Mr. Castillo sent her the balance of the money from his earnings in San Francisco. He also sent them the name of a *coyote* in Mexicali who could get them across the border. Mrs. Castillo traveled by bus with her six children to the U.S. border and went to find the *coyote*. Mr. Castillo and his brother-in-law went down to the border to meet them at the other side.

According to Mrs. Castillo, this was the most difficult part of the journey. They had to wait at the border for twenty-two days before they finally got across. This was because of an increased border patrol presence at the time. There were so many immigration police that a woman with six children would have easily been apprehended. So the *coyote* took them out daily to the border from their hotel in Mexicali to evaluate the situation. Each day they had to return to their hotel. Meanwhile, Mr. Castillo and his brother-in-law were waiting and worrying on the other side. Finally, Mrs. Castillo and the children walked across on a day with less patrol presence. When they got to the other side, they wandered for six or seven hours until they found the car that Mr. Castillo and his brother-in-law had brought to pick them up. Since they didn't know their way around, they had gotten lost in Calexico. Mrs. Castillo says that during the time of the border crossing she had to be constantly wary and alert. She said that there were times when she was approached by drunken men and that she had to keep an impassive face and not engage in conversations with strangers. Mrs. Castillo said that the whole trip was very hard on the children as well. They had to be secured in closed-in places a lot while they were traveling, they became tired of walking, and they had little time to rest and play.

Mr. and Mrs. Castillo returned to San Francisco with their relatives and their children after crossing the border. They settled into a Mission district apartment and, everyone agrees, things have gone relatively smoothly ever since. They are now living in a small two-bedroom apartment in a medium-sized apartment building. Yolanda's sister and her husband and children live in the same building, and they are also friendly with other residents of the building. Nonetheless, the adolescents and younger children do not spend much time playing outside; rather, they engage in a number of activities at home (e.g., toys, books, and television video games). Friends and relatives also visit.

Family members told me that they missed the street corner social life that they were familiar with in Guatemala. Julio told me that he used to play tag and ball games with the children in the streets, and Rodolfo said that their house was next door to a police station, so he was good friends with all of the police. Life here is not as cheerful, says Mr. Castillo. He misses the gaiety of parties and holidays, as he feels that in the United States people like to sleep at night and they do not like loud parties that last late into the night. "We Latinos like parties. Here in this apartment building, people are pretty tolerant. We have put on our own parties, and late into the night too. Nobody ever complains. We even bought fireworks on the fourth of July and set them off at Christmas time." (My family and I attended a confirmation party for the three middle children midway through the interviews. They were confirmed at the local Catholic church, and the party commenced at their home that afternoon and ran late into the evening. The party was quite pleasant, with dancing, lots of beer, wonderful tamales, and party favors for the children.)

Mr. Castillo talks of Guatemala with some nostalgia for the good times. But as he left the country early in 1979, conditions may not have deteriorated to the extent of the street violence that Mrs. Castillo acknowledged. Mr. Castillo also told me that his brothers were talking about coming to the United States for a while because they could no longer make their living as musicians when Ríos Montt instituted the curfew. Musicians generally work in the late afternoons and evenings. Mr. Castillo discouraged them from coming, saying that he has been unable to work in the United States as a musician; there is no money in it. Furthermore, he does not have a marimba.

Early in the interview process, Mr. Castillo told me he was pleased with his ability to find work in the San Francisco area. He works as a plumber, but he laments the fact that it would be too expensive to obtain a license. He also works as a construction worker and remodels houses, as he did in Guatemala. He tells me that he "can do a little bit of everything." He thinks this is a good attitude to bring to work; then you are ready for whatever life brings you. He feels that if a person becomes too specialized, he is also too narrow. He likes to know about every-

thing and try everything. "All work is beautiful. The attitude you bring
to it is the most important." Julio thinks his success in work has to do
with his ability to get along with people and to be open to new things.
Toward the end of the interviewing, Mr. Castillo told me more of his
frustration at not being able to earn more. He said that he feels his
work is creative and professional, but he gets paid only $5 or $6 per
hour, not what he is worth. At this moment, I sensed the internal
pressure he must feel at having to present an optimistic perspective
while the family is living in impoverished conditions.

Mrs. Castillo states that she is happy with her job doing housework.
She prefers working to staying home with the children, as she did in
Guatemala. Besides, she says, life in the United States is so expensive
that it is necessary for her to work. Regarding housework, Yolanda says
that she likes the fact that she goes from house to house to work. She
says she learns a lot that way, seeing how different people live. It is
interesting to her to be exposed constantly to different environments.
She had one or two bad experiences in doing housework when she first
came to the United States. At one time, she and another Latina were
working together in a large home. This other woman would want to
gossip all day long. She finally quit that job because she doesn't like to
be around gossipers. She also quit another job that paid her only $2.75
per hour. Now, she has settled into a routine working six days a week.
Yolanda would like to study English. She started taking adult school
classes when she first came to the United States, but she was frustrated
in that she felt most of the students were not serious. Toward the end
of our interviews she asked me for help in finding English classes.

Mrs. Castillo is in charge of the family finances. She held this
position back in Guatemala as well. She also runs a tight ship vis-à-vis
the household chores. All six children have regular turns with the dishes
and other tasks. It goes very smoothly; no one has to be reminded.
Yolanda's main concern is the debts that the family has incurred. Julio's
attitude toward money is that amassing a lot of money just causes
trouble. He and Yolanda both would like to be able someday to buy a
home in San Francisco. They would eventually like to sell it and take
the profit to Guatemala to buy a home there. This is their dream, but
they have a long way to go. The reality is still the rented two-bedroom
apartment, which is not in good condition. They have made a number
of repairs themselves, and they have tried to get the landlord to get rid
of the mice and cockroaches that are infesting the place. They have
considered withholding rent, but they fear that they will be evicted if they
do so.

The Castillo family members all enjoy good health. When they were new arrivals, the youngest boy, Ernst, was sick a lot with colds and flu. Mrs. Castillo started the family on a regimen of Shaklee vitamins, which she says are expensive but worth it.

School has also been a positive experience for all of the children, including the adolescents. They all get good grades and are well thought of by their teachers and counselors; moreover, they make friends easily in school. Both Mr. and Mrs. Castillo make an effort to involve themselves in school functions and keep in touch with the teachers and counselors for the children. For example, Mrs. Castillo got Mario into the alternative high school that he now attends. She was cleaning house for an administrator who works in the school district office. From this contact she was able to get her son into a school that she felt would be better for him, where there would be fewer bad influences. Mario and his younger brother Rodolfo, who recently enrolled, are both happy with this school. All in all, the children's successful transition to the U.S. schools is probably due to their parents' extensive involvement with these schools.

Of all the children, Mario, the eldest, seems to feel the most pressure from his parents. He is reacting appropriately for his age in showing clear signs of developing autonomy and independence. In taking the bus to school, he does not sit with his brother; rather, he stays with his friends. He has apparently shown an interest in girls, to the point where his mother teases him that he should become a monk. Although Mrs. Castillo has expressed a strong wish that Mario study medicine, he wants to be an architect. (Younger sister Lourdes, age nine, wants to be a doctor.) Finally, in apparent defiance of these serious expectations and in affirmation of his own preference for a less rigid and more relaxed approach to life, he asserts that his hero is the comedian Richard Pryor.

Rodolfo is smaller than Mario and looks younger than his 14 years. He has a very slight build and wears thick glasses. He told me that his favorite teacher was a Latino in middle school who helped the students with discipline. "He called the parents if the students messed up." Rodolfo's goal is to be an airplane mechanic or to go into the army.

Roxanda seems to be a happy and secure 12 year-old girl. She is in middle school, in the sixth grade. Although she shows signs of physical sexual development, she is very petite and demure. She speaks softly but appears to know her own mind. For example, over her father's objections she wants to be a policewoman when she grows up. She plays the violin, is in the gifted program, and gets top grades in all of her subjects. She also is very solicitous and caring of her younger brothers and sisters. All in all, this girl is a charming and bright young adolescent. Her heroine is Wonder Woman.

The Adolescent and Family Culture

The most striking thing about this family is its sense of solidarity and the down-to-earth feeling of security in the home. Both Julio and Yolanda Castillo exude a sense that they are in control (Yolanda even more than Julio), but they do not seem to be heavy-handed about it. Rather, they function as a husband and wife team, with their children closely following their leadership. This can be seen in the testing results in both the FACES test and Family Environment Scale (see Figures 9 and 10). In the FACES test, the family scored as extremely cohesive, even "enmeshed." The parents would like the family to be even more connected, while the children would also like slightly more togetherness. In general, the family members are satisfied with the way things are. On the Family Environment Scale, the family incongruence score was only 10.8, an extremely low score. It indicates that there is very little disagreement in the family as to how they perceive themselves.[9]

What was even more interesting was the process of the interviewing and the testing itself. The parents and children are always home together in the evenings. When I came to interview them, the father and the mother always participated jointly. Even when I asked to interview one of them alone, the other always stayed in the room. The same thing occurred with the adolescents. The parents stayed in the background, and the adolescents wanted to talk to me as a group. This family process was challenged during the paper-and-pencil testing, as each family member was supposed to fill out his or her own individual answer sheet. When I read the test questions, Mrs. Castillo made several attempts to influence the answers of other family members. She did this by reinterpreting the statements of the test in such a way that the answer was implied. I asked her not to do this, but she persisted. Moreover, the rest of the family acquiesced in her covert control. Thus, some questions could be raised about the validity of the test results!

Mr. and Mrs. Castillo and their three oldest children spoke to me of the importance of discipline to the family as a whole. Perhaps the sense of order and smooth family functioning was a skill that aided Mrs. Castillo when she had to cross the border with six small children. But this sense of discipline and order came through in many other ways with this family. The fact that eight people live in a small two-bedroom apartment, and that things were calm, relaxed, and orderly during my visits, was impressive. This family has a system of household duties that is not written down, but everyone knows his or her place down to the six-year-old boy. The family eats together every evening; they attend church together; and there are no arguments about the television, telephone, or record player. There is a lot of family pride. Part of the discipline is in protecting the family from any negative perceptions or criticism of the family. Besides Julio's period of drinking, the accident, and the year of abstinence, there are, no doubt, other family secrets and skeletons (as one might expect from a family in which the father's entire family of origin is connected to the military). Julio's own father was murdered in 1945. Yolanda intimated that secrets must be kept when she mentioned that it was good that the children came to the United States when they were young because if they had been older, their tongues might have been looser.

The adolescents Mario, Rodolfo, and Roxanda are also concerned with supervision and control issues. No doubt their parents' presence in the room during my interviewing skewed their answers to some extent. Mario said that there was a field trip in one of his classes in school. The class was going to go to Chico for three days to learn about agronomy firsthand. He was worried about a lack of supervision and the nature of the other students who would be on the field trip. For this reason, he said, he did not want to attend and he talked to his father about it. His father agreed and he didn't go. Rodolfo told me that his favorite teacher in middle school was a Latino who "taught us discipline." He elaborated by saying that there were a lot of *cholos* in the class and that the teacher would call their parents if they "messed up." Rodolfo has also expressed some interest in going into the army when he is older. As for Roxanda, her ambition is to be a policewoman like one of Charlie's Angels or Wonder Woman. Finally, during the testing, a question was posed to the family about whether family members hit each other. Mario rolled his eyes around, and I noted that all family members but Lourdes answered (on the written sheet) in the affirmative. Both Julio and Yolanda engaged me in discussion later about child abuse laws in the United States and how they felt parents were unduly punished for trying to discipline their children. They had heard of such occurrences in the schools when parents tried to sanction their children for misbehaving, and the parents themselves got into trouble.

The Castillo family scores highest in the Family Environment Scale on achievement and moral-religious emphasis. They see progress as being related to education and adherence to strict moral-religious Catholic values. They also see the United States as a place where the youth have the opportunity to become educated and take their place in an established social order. In Guatemala, Julio said, there is an attitude of enjoying life in the present. He has brought his love of music, partying, and celebration to the United States, and he has even invited non-Latinos to come and party with the family in his home. Thus, he sees himself as a friendly host. But at the same time, he appreciates the pragmatism of the United States and the emphasis on a no-nonsense efficiency. Here in the United States people make better use of their time; thus, "our children can progress more here than they could in Guatemala." Julio said that he talks to his children about these things so they will pick and choose what mixture of U.S. (e.g., pragmatic) and Guatemalan (e.g., present-oriented) customs to follow.

So far, the adolescents have been able to strike an acceptable balance between U.S. and Guatemalan values. While Mario is asking to go out more on his own with his friends and take a more easy-going approach to life (Guatemalan-style), he also has latched on to American music, comedy, and girls. Rodolfo, on the other hand, meets his father at work to do plumbing, construction, and remodeling after school. (Mr. Castillo is training Rodolfo as an apprentice, and Rodolfo helps him by translating for him when needed.) This behavior reflects pragmatic and efficient use of time (U.S. values) and also shows respect and good discipline (Guatemalan values).

Mr. Castillo stresses to his children that they should learn "about everything" so they will be prepared for whatever life brings them. Mrs. Castillo also expresses her interest in learning English and more about U.S. customs. This openness to change is reflected in the FACES family scoring on adaptability. It appears that the family strength is in its cohesion (or enmeshment), leaving it open to an extremely flexible style of adaptation ("chaotic," according to the FACES designation).

Both Mr. and Mrs. Castillo, however, maintain close ties to Guatemala. Mr. Castillo writes letters home quite often, and he talks to his mother on the phone every fifteen days. Mrs. Castillo burns a candle in memory of her father. Symbolically, Yolanda also expressed to me her worries that unbridled obsession with money and progress U.S.-style might lead to disaster befalling her children and economic ruin. She related two recurring dreams: The first one she had before the death of her father and before she brought her children up from Guatemala. In it, her father was standing at a river bank. She was on the other side of the river. He called to her across the river. "Don't leave your children in Guatemala. Take care of them; educate them; they need you." Now that she has brought her children to the United States, she has another recurring dream: This time she is at the same river bank. She can see lots of golden coins in the water. She goes into the water and picks them up. When she comes back out of the water, she looks at the coins and sees that they are worthless. She laughed when she told me what she thought this dream meant: "More poverty!"

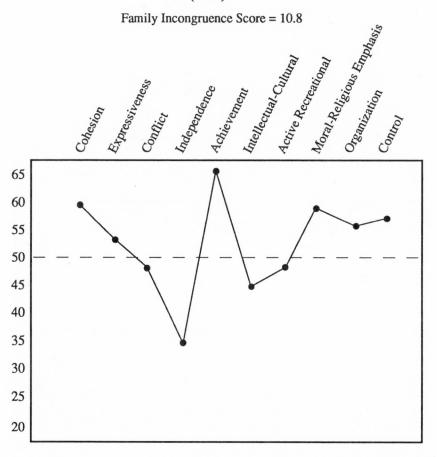

FIGURE 9 - The Castillo Family

Family Environment Scale

(FES)

Family Incongruence Score = 10.8

FIGURE 10 - The Castillo Family

Family Adaptability and Cohesion Scale
(FACES)

Family Discrepancy Score = 2.5

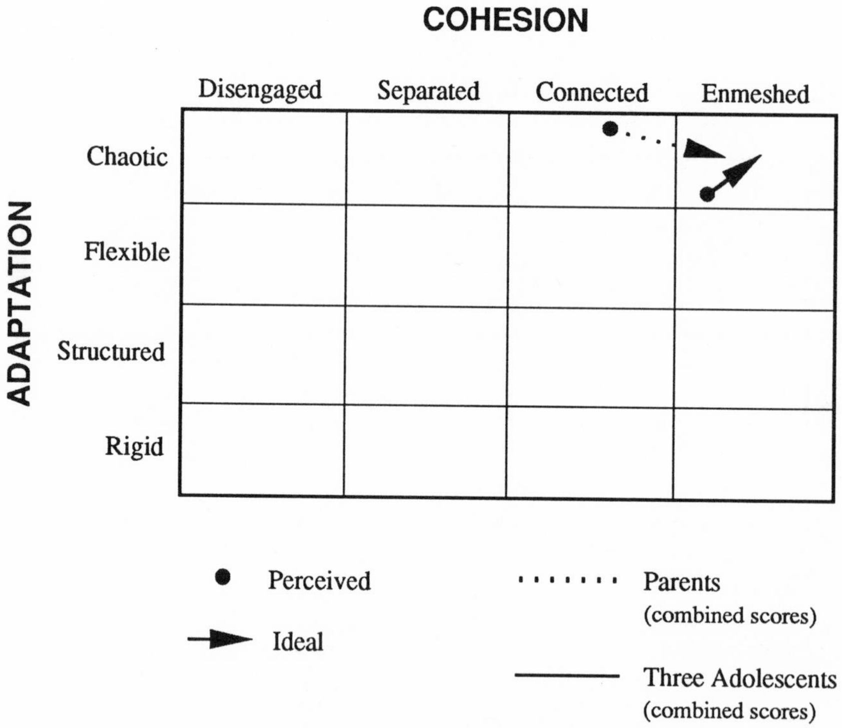

COHESION

	Disengaged	Separated	Connected	Enmeshed
Chaotic				
Flexible				
Structured				
Rigid				

ADAPTATION

● Perceived   • • • • • • Parents (combined scores)

➤ Ideal   ——— Three Adolescents (combined scores)

MIGRATION AND COPING

THE MEANING OF MIGRATION

The experience of migrating families can be analyzed on three levels:
(1) salient historical-structural conditions; (2) immediate and precipitating causes and circumstances: and (3) personal and family reasons for
emigration (Arizpe 1975). The first level sets the stage for the decision
to migrate; the second provides the direction and, to some extent, the
script; and the third level takes into account the individual actors and
their unique styles of working together in an ensemble.

Historical-Structural Conditions

All of the families in this study are products of the history of
Guatemala and the structural conditions of Guatemalan society.
Although there are no mechanical cause-and-effect relationships between
these factors and the family migrations, they do provide the context in
which the families' leavetaking occurs.

What is unique about Guatemalans is their hidden and restrained
identity: Many are blatant Hispanophiles, and others are members of an
Indian ethnic community or hold to traits or memories of a linguistic and
ethnic Indian loyalty. In relation to other Latin American nationalities
and the U.S. experience, Guatemalans demonstrate a cautious and
formal distancing in interpersonal interaction that is at once European
and Indian. This behavior is a consequence of the historical-structural
conditions of Guatemalan society, as well as of the status of Guatemalan
migrants once they come to the United States.

The four central conditions of Guatemalan culture and society that set
the stage for the family migrations are the following: (1) demographic
growth among the poor and Indian peoples, (2) land-use policy of

competitive allocation, (3) U.S. ambivalence toward investment and military involvement, and (4) long-standing social and cultural schisms and inequities among the Guatemalan people themselves.

Guatemala is undergoing a population explosion, especially within the Indian sector. The rate of natural increase of Indians has surpassed that of Ladinos in the population at large; this is a reversal of the demographic relationship between the two groups that has existed since the sixteenth century. Along with the changing population ratio is the problem of widespread childhood malnutrition and land scarcity. Land-use policy maintains inequitable allocation of land for the benefit of a small minority of elite landowners, foreign investors, and the military. Pervasive intervention by the United States and other foreign countries in the running of Guatemala's economy, political process, military, and popular culture occurs in response to short-lived and short-sighted political pressures and export economy needs.

The social consequences of this type of political economy have been twofold. First, large sections of the mostly Indian population have been uprooted in a genocidal militarization of the countryside. Second, accelerated and forced processes of Ladinoization and urbanization are creating new and multiple loyalties and dependencies. Such trends are heightening ethnic and related social schisms and tensions throughout the country.

Immediate Circumstances: The Push and the Pull

The second level of analysis poses this question: What are the immediate and precipitating causes and circumstances for the migration of Guatemalan families—the "push" and "pull" factors? In this intermediate level of analysis, the macrostructural context is broken down further into specific events and the social structure of the events.

The relationship between the first and second levels of analysis may be shown in the following illustration: Most of the families in this study, although they are in the mid-life stage of their life cycle, do not own property in Guatemala. Although it is clear that the macrostructural conditions of demographic growth and land-use policy have affected these families indirectly in their lack of land ownership, other factors have more immediately precipitated their moves. That is, political and economic factors such as paramilitary activity, inflation, and low wages have exacerbated the problematic previous conditions.

It is at this point that many studies of migration and resettlement categorize migrants as either free or forced to move. Especially for these families, I have chosen to take a different approach. I see the push factors impelling people to move and the pull factors, or the strategic paths migrants take, as two sides of the same coin. The six families in this study are neither solely victims (of events or class structure at home) nor solely goal-oriented individuals (who are maximizing their options through taking a risk in a new setting); rather, they are both of these. In the Chavez family, the differing perceptions of the migration experience between the father and the adolescents is an example of this situation.

How do these second-level causes apply to the families in this study? There are two pull factors that have brought Guatemalan immigrants and refugees into the United States. They are the same factors that have inspired generations of immigrant predecessors from all over the world to come to the United States: (1) the perception of the United States as an economically more viable place to live than their homeland, and (2) a connection with a migration chain. All of the Guatemalan immigrants I interviewed expected to find work here and better wages to support their families. In Guatemala City, information was generally available about the United States through newspapers, word of mouth, and television. To some, the image of the United States had taken on a mythic quality; others simply saw it as an option to make some money.

The second pull factor, connection to a migration chain, is especially salient for the Guatemalan families in this study. Four of the six families that came to the San Francisco Bay Area chose to do so because they had adult relatives living in the area. In these four cases, the adult relatives encouraged them to come and helped to feed and house them when they arrived, as well as giving them leads for finding jobs. In the Menchú-Franzi family, a female friend helped out the mother who came up first. Only in the Navarro family did the mother come up without the help of a relative or friend; it was, however, not her first trip to the United States—she had come up earlier with family assistance.

There are three primary push factors that have led to the immigration of the families in this study to the United States. They are (1) inflation, unemployment, and low wages, (2) political tension, repression, rebellion, and massacres throughout the homeland, and (3) the 1976 earthquake and its aftermath.

Inflation, unemployment, and low wages constitute the first push factor. All six of the families in the study stated unequivocally that they came to the United States because the wages they received in Guatemala were extremely low and they could not adequately provide for their families. They recognized that inflation, low wages, and unemployment were major precipitants of their decision to move. Structurally, all but one of the families in the study fall into the working poor category. The one middle-class family in the study (the Walter family) has both parents as members of the "liberal professions" in Guatemala, the second stream of migrants that is leaving Guatemala. None of the families in the study is completely destitute, as traveling as far as the San Francisco Bay Area presumes a certain amount of financial resources that the most desperate would never possess.

The second push factor, equally important, is political violence. All six of the families in the study cited political violence as a key determinant of their moving from Guatemala. Although political violence has been a way of life in Guatemala throughout its history, most people do not remember it ever being as bad as it is now. Family members often commented that it was dangerous to work or to engage in normal activities such as going to school, going to market, conversing with strangers, even leaving the confines of their houses, for fear of terrorism. Some stated that certain occupations such as teaching, studying at the university, doing church work, or being a journalist, were open targets. Even being a musician was impossible when Ríos Montt instituted the curfews. The one family from the rural frontier with Mexico (the Chavez family) had first-hand experience with helicopter strafing and burning of villages and crops, which was making farming also a dangerous occupation.

A serendipitous historical finding in relation to the effect of political events on migration patterns emerged among the families in this study. In all of the families, one or more members were recent migrants to Guatemala City at or after the time of the aborted electoral revolution of 1944-1945. It seems that expectations were raised at that time for many families, and that the families' hopes were subsequently thwarted.

The third push factor influencing families to come to the United States was the 1976 earthquake. Four of the six families cited the earthquake as strongly affecting their decision to leave Guatemala. Many of the families' homes were destroyed, and with the economic chaos that followed, their abilities to make a living were seriously impaired. In the Walter family, the father started drinking heavily "after the earthquake." In the García family, the six-year-old daughter suffered from *susto* as a consequence. In two other families (the Navarro and Castillo families), the mothers made their decisions to come to the United States to stay shortly after the earthquake and its devastation.

Table 1 is a summary of the immediate and precipitating causes and circumstances of the migration of families in this study, both the pull and the push factors. It lists the first two levels of analysis of the meaning of migration for the families in the study. The chart provides the context for the third level of analysis of family migration that follows, personal and family reasons for emigration.

TABLE 1
Historical-Structural Conditions of Migration
and Immediate Circumstances of Migration

Historical-Structural Conditions
* Demographic growth among the poor and Indian people * Land–use policy of competitive allocation * U.S. ambivalence toward investment and military involvement * Social and cultural schisms and inequities among the Guatemalan people

Immediate Circumstances
Pull Factors * United States is perceived as economically more viable; family members expect to find work here and earn enough to support the family * Connection with a migration chain Push Factors * Inflation, unemployment, low wages * Political tension, repression, rebellion, and massacres * 1976 earthquake

Personal and Family Reasons for Emigration

Personal and family reasons for emigration constitute the third and most difficult level of analysis. This is because, as Sluzki notes, recently arrived migrants are inured in the "overcompensation" stage of their migration. They feel uneasy in their new environment, strangers in an alien culture. Consequently, they often find it difficult to explain the personal significance of their decision at a time (after arrival) when the struggle to survive is so intense (Sluzki 1979). Tobias concurs in his observation that "old talk" may be the acceptable cover story that a migrant may glibly recite when asked about his or her reason for emigrating, while "the truth" can better be determined by talking to the migrant's friends and family (Tobias 1976). The research methods used in this study lend themselves to such examination of "the truth." Earlier in this book I made reference to the Roshoman approach to families' decisions to emigrate as well as to the Latino cultural style of circling around a point rather than bluntly discussing a sensitive and personal issue. Thus, the question "Why did you decide to move to the United States?" was asked of various family members; their differing responses were all included in the analysis. Enough data were derived from such a technique that I was better able to see patterns and to infer connections between specific family and personal crises and the subsequent decisions to move than I would have if only one family member was interviewed.

TABLE 2
Personal and Family Reasons for Emigration

* Family member may be target for political terrorism or close family member has already been tortured or murdered
* Estrangement from mate (spouse or sweetheart) or family
* Attempted reunification with family members
* Dreams of progress and hope for future
* Medical expenses
* Attempt to buy a home
* Threats of imprisonment (for debts) or revenge (for gang activities)

The clusters listed in Table 2 are the most frequently mentioned personal and family reasons for emigration. Commonly cited personal and family reasons for leaving Guatemala for the United States confirm the importance of social relations and family dynamics. Spousal or family estrangement, attempts toward reunification, family support and encouragement in the fulfillment of hopes and dreams, and family burdens of medical expenses for sick relatives are reasons often given for emigration.

In the Menchú-Franzi family, the mother was estranged and, subsequently, divorced from her husband. This left her pessimistic about her future in Guatemala. Her son, Miguel, came to the United States partly because he wanted to escape from a sweetheart who was pressuring him to marry her. The mother in the García family also left partly to get away from her overcritical siblings and a deceiving lover, the father of three of her children. Similarly, Dolores, the teenage mother in the Chavez family, sought to escape an unhappy love affair through her odyssey to the United States. At the same time that they were cutting ties at home, all of the families successfully reunited with their children (and, often, spouses) in the United States. For most, this was preferable to maintaining the labor migration and concomitant enforced family separation that many had initially undertaken.

Family support and encouragement was a key factor mentioned by most families as instrumental in raising their spirits for the arduous adventure of emigration. As important as emotional support were gifts or loans of cash and/or promise of aid in acquiring legal status from relatives who were already U.S. citizens or who had their residency.

The necessity for earning money to pay medical bills for sick relatives was often cited as a motivating factor. Usually the relatives were elderly parents.

Two families were attempting to purchase their own homes. The García family was already making payments on a home in Guatemala, and the Castillo family was working toward this goal. In the analysis of the meaning of migration at the first and second levels (historical-structural conditions and immediate circumstances), lack of land ownership was mentioned as a widespread concern, with inflation and low wages exacerbating the problem. Here, at the personal and family level of decision making, the migrant families were attempting to confront the dilemma by raising the capital in the United States toward the goal of home purchase. In both cases, they appeared to be unsuccessful. Ms. García had to sell her home to finance the emigration of her daughters, and the Castillo family could barely make ends meet. It is significant that reunification takes precedence over the goal of home ownership. The cost of family reunification makes home ownership unlikely for these migrant families in the foreseeable future despite their overwhelming efforts.

Beyond the family dynamics, the most common personal reason given for leaving Guatemala was vulnerability to political terrorism. In all of the families, one or more members were especially vulnerable. In the Walter family, both husband and wife were middle-class "liberal" professionals—he a journalist, she a teacher. They felt that their professions put them in a position in which they could be attacked. The father in the Chavez family had been an organizer for the Christian Democratic party in the border province of San Marcos. This set him up as a leader and potential victim. In the Menchú family, two sons were murdered by political assassins; this left one remaining 19-year-old son who naturally felt that he could be next. Finally, the Navarro family had already had experience with the political kidnapping and torture of an uncle and the burning of the home of a cousin. The oldest son never acknowledged to me any sense of his own vulnerability, but his mother hinted that he may have been somehow involved in the conflict. Even the other two families that gave me no indications of any specific concern gave clues that they too may have felt in danger. The mother in the García family was an important distributor of foodstuff to the poor through the Catholic Church. Upon moving to the United States, she rejected her ties to the Catholic Church by joining an evangelical church even though she did not particularly like the services. The father in the Castillo family (whose own father was murdered under mysterious circumstances) came from a family of military men. Although they may deny it, such social roles put the Castillo and García families automatically at some political risk.

These and other personal and family reasons that were cited may be only the tip of the iceberg. Occasionally, family members seemed fearful of revealing complete biographical information. This was manifested by the person speaking in an extremely low voice, speaking glibly in a monotone without thinking through complex questions, coughing a lot, or displaying a number of nervous mannerisms. Suspiciousness and psychic numbing are coping mechanisms that families and family members sometimes fall back on in talking to outsiders. Often, people who have experienced traumatic stress deny or forget unpleasant things that have happened to them. In a couple of instances, members actually told me directly that the data were incomplete because of selective amnesia ("It's better to forget unpleasant things"). Only in questions about recurring dreams did many family members begin to explore the range of rich and symbolic meaning that migration has for them. The significance of the dream material will be discussed at the end of the section on marital and family conflict.

HOW FAMILIES COPE

Although families in this study vary, they display common characteristic family migration experiences and coping styles. I have used the ABCX model as an analytical tool to aid in sorting out responses about the typical migration experience. A basic family profile emerges from the data, as well as idiosyncratic family themes. Typical forms of social support and social interaction are also found within the families.

Family Coping Using the ABCX Model

The Stress Event or Hardship (A)

All of the families in this study are faced with more stress events or hardships than the act of migrating presents per se. I have already illuminated many of these hardships in my description of the historical-structural conditions as a stage or field of action, the immediate circumstances as the script, and the personal family dimensions as a dynamic interaction of actors in an ensemble. These simultaneous conditions, circumstances, and intimate interactions have triggered the dramas of the various emigrations. In addition to this background similarity, most of the families in the study have in common the fact that they have entered the United States illegally and in defiance of official U.S. policy. During resettlement, they have endured privations, struggled with the language barrier, and suffered other threats to their self-esteem. Furthermore, the presence of teenagers in the household creates more difficulties (Erikson 1954).

First, back home, families in this study have not just one but many crises: They have undergone marital and family estrangement, political terror, bouts of alcoholism, catastrophic illnesses, childbearing without paternal support, piling up of debts, and family deaths, including murders. Each of these crises alone might prove a sufficient environmental stress to threaten the emotional stability and health of any ordinary family.

Second, four of the families in the study have made a traumatic overland journey in which they had to enter the United States clandestinely. In two of these cases, there is no resolution in sight for the anxiety of illegal status in this country. Undocumented status means that the family members must always remain somewhat hidden, maintaining a low profile in the host community, thereby depriving the children of access to education past high school or age 18.[1] In addition, there is always the fear of detection and deportation.

Third, the conditions of resettlement in the United States have been frustrating, humiliating, and lonely for many of the families. Inability to communicate in English and an unstable and insecure job market intensify the pressure. In Sluzki's scheme, all six families are function-ing in the third stage, or "period of overcompensation." Two families are approaching the fourth stage, or "period of decompensation" (Sluzki 1979). For example, the Walter family is undergoing severe marital strife, and the husband is drinking excessively. There is a potential for child abuse and further escalation of difficulties. In the Menchú-Franzi family, there has been much conflict between the stepchildren of one parent and the stepchildren of the other parent. This may lead shortly to the family splitting up, the children leaving home, and the reor-ganization of the family.

Finally, a critical stress on the families is the presence of teenagers. All of the families were chosen for this study because they have one or more adolescents in their households. By definition, the "mid-life" or "child-launching" stage in the life cycle is a period of family difficulty. Marital strain is a common occurrence. The youth are thinking of leaving the family of origin and beginning a new family of their own. This situation of strain on the marital dyad and of the "emancipation" of the youth may be felt more or less strongly and manifested differently in different cultures, but the issues are common in many societies (Davis 1940; Erikson 1954; Olson et al. 1983b; Carter and McGoldrick 1988).

In the families I studied, there is the additional strain of having undergone a protracted family separation. The precariousness of reunification under these circumstances is apparent. Parents have often been separated from each other and their children for many years. To some extent, this is a continuation of the *internado* system of education in Guatemala in which children of all classes are often placed in boarding schools while their parents work. In fact, however, the *internado* system in Guatemala has broken down substantially. Families no longer have the professional, institutional, and financial supports and stability to follow the traditional forms of child rearing. In many cases, the youth are left on their own or are unceremoniously placed with dubiously willing relatives, neighbors, or even strangers who are overburdened with their own problems. Among the families in this study, parents were working in the United States for a time before they brought their children here to live. In most cases, parents were unhappy with living conditions for their children when they themselves were not present to watch out for them. In addition, there are other problems following family reunification. Sometimes the youth arrive expecting more freedom and less controls than they now have. Or, they long for more care and guidance than their families are able to provide. Parents and their children often want to make up for lost time; it is sometimes too late for this.

All of these stressful events and hardships cause many of the families in the study to experience a "pile-up" or overload of difficulties. This taxes their abilities to develop coping strategies.

Resources (B)

The primary resources that the families in this study use are the support of extended family members and churches—particularly the evangelical churches. In addition, family members lean heavily on the nuclear unit.

Study families followed this pattern: Most had relatives or friends living in the United States before they came themselves. Generally, this relative or friend helped one member of the family with transportation costs, housing, and finding a job. Once the first family member was established and working, she or he made plans to bring the rest of the family in a chain migration. In these families, the U.S. relative had or was obtaining legal residency and could petition for residency for his or her relatives. This situation often puts the families in the position of total dependence on the good will of one relative—causing tension in at least two of the study families. In the Walter family, for example, the father-in-law has refused to petition for the rest of the family that are now here; they must stay in limbo until he changes his mind.

Besides the extended family, there is one other important resource that most of the families use: the church. Three of the families in the study are members of evangelical Pentecostal churches, institutions that play a strong role for newcomers from Guatemala. Such congregations envelop new arrivals and provide a sense of security and caring for many families who feel lonely, insecure, and wounded by the traumatic experiences they have undergone.

Perhaps because of their tenuous legal status in the country and also because of limited time, families do not seek out many other social network resources besides the family and the church. The three Catholic families in the study attend church regularly, but they have no involvement in church social clubs and organizations similar to that of the

Pentecostal families. (One family, the Navarro family, did ask for cash assistance from a Catholic refugee program.) Although individual family members do have both peer and patronage connections with people they have met through school and work, they generally have little time for socializing or recreation.

Perceptions (C)

In the study of migration, migrant adaptation has often been described in a peculiarly asocial manner. The migrant is seen as an individual rather than as an integral part of a social and (in this case) familial system. Acculturation studies generally do not delineate the context in which stress occurs, resources are utilized, and perceptions are held. By taking the family as the basic unit, this study broadens the perception of the migrant and puts the family system into the cognitive map.

For the families in this study, perception of the migration and resettlement experience has been marred by a good deal of conflict. Families show little cohesion, and there is low congruence in the opinions of family members. Four out of the six families (Walter, Menchú-Franzi, Chavez, and García) indicated the most disagreement.[2] Among the four most conflicted families, there is a wide split in attitudes and expectations about Guatemala and about how to proceed in the United States. It is instructive to examine how these conflicting notions are found in each of the four families.

In the Walter family, the covert political conflict between the husband and wife has taken on the proportions of growing marital disharmony.

The blended Menchú-Franzi family is culturally split on attitudes about Guatemala between the U.S.-born children and the Guatemalan-born children who are recent immigrants. The sentiments are so intense that the family cannot tolerate living together under the same roof much longer.

The large Chavez family consists of eleven children, most of whom are young adults, newly married and living in the United States. The younger siblings are still in Guatemala with their mother and recently returned father. Conflict in this family is not overt; rather, what is occurring is a gradual separation among the family members, with the ones living in the United States growing farther and farther apart from the rest of the family in Guatemala.

In the García family, there is an ethos of controlled assimilation. Ms. García states that the United States is "much better than Guatemala" (more freedom), but ironically she behaves in a very controlling way toward her children. There is a lot of fighting, and there is no sense of family unity. Nostalgia for Guatemala occasionally and inadvertently creeps into the conversation.

In general, all of the families define the hardships that they have faced and are facing by allowing some members in the family to take on an active, future-oriented, positive approach to their experience. In the same family, though, there is usually at least one family member who takes on the role of mourner for the family. This member (or members) talks a lot about Guatemala and is more critical of the United States than the other family members. Families thus integrate both positive and negative perceptions of the migration experience, inadvertently achieving a kind of balanced perception for the family as a whole.

Family Experience (X)—The Process of Coping

The families in the study felt the experience of migration and resettlement to be more or less devastating depending on the interaction of the stressors, resources, and perceptions involved. The families that were inundated by a number of hardships tended to pull apart in a more centrifugal fashion. For example, the Chavez and García families were those with the most stressful events; these families had a disengaged style of coping. Those with fewer environmental stressors pulled together more. For instance, the Castillo family had the least hardships; it was also the family with the most cohesive coping style.

Resources available to the families have proved to be both a blessing and a liability. Extended family members and the church groups to which families belong exert pressures and demands of their own in addition to providing succor and aid for new arrivals. In many cases, the reciprocal demands of relatives and churches take on a negative rather than supportive character.

In terms of resources of the internal family system, leadership has proved to be a crucial determinant of how the families cope. Parental figures who were united in developing a uniform ideological rationale for migration and set of expectations for resettlement also made for a more cohesive style of adapting (as in the Castillo family). On the other hand, if there was diffuse and confusing leadership in the family, or if the parental figures could not take instrumental or expressive control of the family (as in the García, Menchú-Franzi, Walter, and Chavez families), a more disengaged style tended to develop and family members were more autonomous entities, with less sense of strong family organization and cohesion. In most cases, mothers played stronger roles in relation to family unity than did fathers.

Emotionally, most families in the study are internally divided in their sentiments toward the United States and Guatemala: These families have also taken on a disengaged behavioral style of coping. For example, these families do not take the trouble to eat meals together or generally gather together as a unit. In fact, mealtimes can precipitate family battles if they do try to eat together. The Menchú-Franzi family was eating dinner together one night when an argument ensued, plates were thrown around, threats were made, and the neighbors even called the police.

Family Cultural Styles and Themes

Beyond the ABCX model, a number of themes emerge from each family that characterize their own idiosyncratic styles of coping. These themes express the ethos of each particular family with respect to migration at this point in the family life cycle; the themes also suggest issues that migrating families in general might face.

Conflict, Adventure, and Death: Ido de sentido *(Menchú-Franzi family)*

The Guatemalan- and U.S.-born children have split this family in two. A strong adventurous spirit has been dulled by a sense of sadness and loss following the deaths of so many young men (four, two murdered) in the family.

Success and Sacrifice (Walter family)

High achievement in this family is accomplished along with a great deal of pain. Poor health, the father's excessive drinking, physical beatings of the children, and a marital "civil war" are the sacrifices that the family has made.

Control and Freedom: Losing Hope (Chavez family)

This family has found a new set of dangers in the city in comparison to the dangers they faced in their rural home. The changes they have undergone from Indian origins to Ladino customs and values to a new immigrant identity tax their ability to persevere as a family. This adjustment has strained male and female role expectations, making control and freedom central concerns for them.

Assimilation: America and the Soul (García family)

This is a lonely family with assimilation as their professed goal. Follwing the American dream is proving somewhat hollow for them as they keep feeling a surprising sense of nostalgic and romantic attachment to Guatemala and a need to control the rate of assimilation after all.

Familism, Nationalism, and Obligation (Navarro family)

This family is strongly tied to the extended family in Guatemala, to religious values, and to a sense of duty and pride in their traditions. Their U.S. adaptation has been pragmatic and tentative.

Solidarity and Discipline (Castillo family)

Unity has been the key to this family's ready adaptation to change in the United States. A strong sense of discipline prevails as the family redefines hardships as opportunities and works to build for the children's futures.

Centripetal and Centrifugal Coping Styles

In reviewing the data on the six families, it is apparent that some of them develop a close and cohesive adaptive style but that most take on a more disengaged, separated adaptive mode. The central finding in this study is that most of the families cope with the early stage of the migration process through disengagement and conflict. Although the casual outside observer may see these families as close and supportive of each other, family members themselves do not perceive their family relations in this way. Family separation and tension seem to be concomitants of this overcompensation phase. Change and adjustment are necessary for them to achieve their goals, and the pace of adaptation becomes an issue as family members often clash over how Guatemala and the United States are perceived and over the meaning of the migration experience to the family.

I call the two adaptive coping styles taken by the six families centripetal and centrifugal based on the work of Stierlin and Ravenscroft, who use the terms "binding" and "expelling" (Stierlin and Ravenscroft 1972). They describe two extreme types of transactional modes between parents and adolescents—binding (centripetal) and expelling (centrifugal).

In the centripetal mode, parents interact to keep the adolescent tied closely to the parental orbit. Parents may intrude on the youth's definitions of his or her feelings and actions. In the case of the Castillo family, it was difficult for me to administer the family evaluation testing, for example. The mother was constantly interrupting to interpret the items to her adolescent children with an inferred "correct" answer.

In the centrifugal mode, the parents give confused, inconsistent, or rejecting messages to their children. Adolescents feel neglected and pushed into premature separation and disengagement. The García family provides a good illustration of ambivalence: Ms. García states that she wants her daughters to enjoy the freedom of the United States, but at the same time she behaves in a very controlling way with them.

There is a correlation between how these families perceive the migration experience and the results of the family evaluation testing. The most conflicted families (Walter, Menchú-Franzi, Chavez, and García) have very similar scores (see Table 3). In the FACES test, the same four families are disengaged in their approach to the migration experience. These same families show scores ranging from 11.2 to 23.2 in the amount of discrepancy they indicate between their perceptions about actual family cohesion and adaptability and their desires for what would be the ideal family cohesion and adaptation. Most noticeably, these families do show unanimity on one issue—their dissatisfaction with the status quo and their wish to increase their cohesion and adaptability. They would like to increase their ability to adapt or have more flexible family rules. To a somewhat lesser extent, they would also like to develop closer family bonds, especially the teenagers in the Navarro, Menchú-Franzi, and Walter families.[3]

In at least three of the families (Walter, Menchú-Franzi, and García)[4] a similar pattern is found in the scoring on the Family Environment Scale. The pattern includes: high scores in (1) achievement, (2) moral-religious orientation, and (3) conflict; low scores in (1) independence, (2) cohesion, and (3) recreation. Struggling and overcompensating in their desire to compete in the U.S. marketplace, the families are caught in a dilemma of cultural discontinuity; the consequent moral-religious quest for meaning and the stress of family reorganization throw many into intra-family conflict.

Thus, there is a characteristic profile of the Guatemalan immigrant family with adolescents at this stage in the migration process. The profile is one of a centrifugal-style, conflicted, achievement-oriented, religious family that is not very cohesive. Family members are frustrated and feel held back in their desire to make the necessary changes to succeed in the United States. They have little time and energy for independent or recreational pursuits, and instead, they feel compelled to work at a survival level.

The two other families that do not fit the paradigm have found other methods to cope, centripetal-style, with the migration experience.[5] In the Navarro family, the three family members all maintain strict loyalty to the extended family and to Guatemala. Their roles are all well organized and based on tradition and obligation. The mother carries the role of mourner for the family. The older brother is the caretaker for the mother. And the youngest brother wants to return to Guatemala as an expert agronomist. The Navarros have not established a network here in the United States. They have been living in temporary rooms rented out of people's houses. Psychologically, they are still living in Guatemala.

The Castillo family does not follow the paradigm of conflict and disengagement either. They have found yet another way to cope with the migration experience. They have chosen to perceive the experience as a positive one. Theirs is a good example of cognitive coping in that

TABLE 3
Characteristic Profile of Guatemalan Families in the Study

Family Environment Scale (Walter, Menchú-Franzi, García families)

High Scores
    (1) Achievement
    (2) Moral-religious orientation
    (3) Conflict
 	
Low Scores
    (1) Independence
    (2) Cohesion
    (3) Recreation

Family Adaptability and Cohesion Scale (all families)

Average Family Discrepancy Scores
    Cohesion = 10.9 ("Disengaged wanting separation")
    Adaptation = 12.9 ("Rigid wanting flexible")

the parents have taken on the idea of change as a good thing; they say it makes a person stronger and better. The family is also quite united, by U.S. standards, even enmeshed, and, unlike the other families, they see themselves as extremely flexibly adapted. The strong sense of family security comes because the parents unite in providing leadership and guidance and in seeking the best for their children. Although the bonding may be somewhat oppressive at times, it is apparently a good solution for this family at a difficult phase in the life cycle and the migration process.

The Role of the Evangelical Church

In the profile of the typical Guatemalan family in this study (adapting, religious, conflicted, disengaged), the tendency is toward the centrifugal style of coping. This centrifugal style has two other important social and interactional correlates: (1) existence of marital/family estrangement, and (2) reliance on the church.

The Catholic Church always has been a vital institution throughout Latin America, and it is no less so in Guatemala. However, ever since Catholic priests, bishops, and nuns in Guatemala took on a more activist stance of organizing Indians and Ladinos in terms of community interests, the Catholic Church has been a target of violence. More and more well-financed evangelical Pentecostal missions and missionaries have been imported to Guatemala, many of them from the United States. These churches are also popular in the United States, and many families who are new arrivals seek them out.

The three families in this study who have been involved with the Pentecostal churches have taken a number of different styles of interaction in relation to the services and the reciprocal demands of the churches. The Walter family has become totally involved. They have taken on leadership roles in the church, and they attend meetings and services almost every day. The adolescent daughter's best friend is the daughter of the preacher, and the mother teaches a Spanish class for church members. The Chavez family maintains only peripheral involvement after initially of attending a lot of meetings and revivals. The church was helpful in finding work for the father, and he kept up his attendance. But other family members have become "too busy" to go, and the adolescent daughter tells me that she doesn't like all the fuss and noise that they make when they are speaking in tongues. The García family joined the church after arriving in the United States on the suggestion of the oldest daughter (who was already married and out of the home). The mother has become disenchanted with the church and how they "take your children away from you." Now the family does not attend any church.

Involvement in the evangelical church may have some connection with the search by many Guatemalans and Guatemalan immigrants for an ideology, an identity, and an emotional release for the hidden pain so many carry with them. The expressive and cathartic rituals and nurturing structure may provide some meaning to their lives at a time of so many losses. While the three Catholic families in the study attend church regularly and maintain their respect for Catholic beliefs and traditions, they have no involvement in social clubs and organizations connected with the church. The rise and fall of Guatemalan evangelist president Ríos Montt may have a lot to do with the pragmatics of engagement and disengagement with the evangelical church. The evangelical phenomenon may also be a function of a certain stage in the migration process in which families are searching for attachment and a new set of symbols to explain what is happening in their lives. As the families become more settled in the United States and as they feel somewhat more stable, they may become disillusioned with certain aspects of the evangelical style. Factors such as the aggressive demeanor, demands for time and money, lack of respect for status and authority, and unreserved displays of emotion (e.g., speaking in tongues) are eventually seen by many families as culturally incongruent and unacceptable.

Furthermore, the significant correlation in relation to choice of religious affiliation turns out to be centrifugal coping style. The three families that have joined the evangelical churches have been the highly adapting, conflicted, disengaged type that most clearly follow the profile of the typical Guatemalan family. The Catholic families do not fit the paradigm: Their tendency is toward a more centripetal style of coping in the United States. (There is one exception, the still Catholic Menchú-Franzi family. Testing indicates that this family follows the centrifugal profile of the typical immigrant family.)

In general, though, the families that are the closest and most cohesive are Catholic. The families in which unity is lacking are more likely to be evangelical. I would propose that the evangelical church attracts these disunited families by providing a ready-made superstructure or pseudo-family in which they can turn their lives over to the church. The intensity of both time and emotional involvement suggests that this institution provides a more corporate and total haven for families that are without direction or leadership. The Catholic church does not appear to take on this sort of role for families belonging to it. Instead, they rely on each other and the centripetal copying style of adaptation. This may also be a carryover from the Guatemalan scene in which

Catholic organizations are targets for terrorist death squads. A centripetal coping style maintaining strict boundaries between the family and outside institutions may better ensure survival under such conditions.

Marital and Family Conflict

A tendency toward the centrifugal coping style is also related to problems of marital and family estrangement and reunification. Families with adolescents who come to the United States from Guatemala bring their family histories with them in the form of memories, learned social roles, and styles of behavior. The United States provides a different environment and a different set of cultural expectations in and of themselves quite conducive to marital and family conflict. Yet the families experience the new setting and new demands as a continuation of the struggle they left behind. With new rules and new organization to contend with, new conflicts emerge as well.

Family histories related by the six families are full of stories of inequality and domination, usually by Ladino men in relation to Ladina women. In Guatemala, Ladino husbands and fathers have traditionally played the most important economic role in the household. They have been the migrant laborers, leaving their wives at home to care for the family. The pattern was set at the time of the conquest of Guatemala when Spanish men were the travelers and conquerors. Indian women were the conquered, and Indian men were superfluous, except as forced laborers. Indian women served as buffers to ease the conflict between the dominant Spanish society and the dominated Indian communities.

Machismo[6] and *marianismo*[7] are the extreme sorts of masculine aggressiveness and female submission that are commonly encountered as inequality and domination-submission patterns become learned behavior (Stevens 1973). In the Guatemalan families studied here, this historical Ladino behavioral residue was often apparent. I became particularly sensitive to it in my work with the Chavez family. Mr. Chavez was an older Indian *campesino* who had lost all of his power and social status; he was put in a position in which his wife was unavailable, he could not find steady work, and he was being interviewed by an independent, nonsubmissive, Guatemalan-American, light-skinned woman. Since I did not fit his definition of a decent home-oriented, submissive Ladina woman, I must therefore be an indecent American woman. At one point, during our final interview, Mr. Chavez made a weak attempt at sexually aggressive behavior toward me, as the cultural discontinuity was too much for him at that difficult time.

The United States offers a different atmosphere for migrating Guatemalan families with respect to traditional husband and wife roles. For example, the emergence of a sexual differential among the first migrants in the family migration chain is a notable finding in this study. Many school and agency personnel with whom I spoke assumed that the men were the first to come to the United States and that they subsequently sent for their wives and families. But in five out of six of the families, a female member of the extended or nuclear family was the first to enter the United States, with the rest of the family following either all together or in chain fashion. In only one instance did the father enter the country first. This family is the one middle-class professional family in the group. The father was following after other relatives, some of whom had U.S. parentage.

Thus, among the working poor families in the study, the woman appears to be the one who takes the initiative to enter the United States (Cohen 1979). She generally comes up first to survey the situation, make some money, and make a decision about bringing up the rest of the family. Later, if possible, the children come. Women also commit themselves to staying in the United States sooner than do the men. The study families thus corroborate statistics on recent trends in Hispanic immigration to the United States. That is, according to statistics on recent cohorts (Massey and Schnabel 1983), Central and South American immigrants are mostly women.

There are a number of possible reasons for the preponderance of women entering the United States first and deciding to stay more quickly than the men. First, the social history of the Guatemalan family has been overlaid with racial and class conflict and domination. Family relations have existed in a political economy in which migration and family separation have proved to be necessary survival strategies. In a context of separation and inequality, the family unit based on the husband and wife as a team becomes precarious and estrangement is common. In many cases, marriage does not take place at all. The cultural role of the wife and her mother as the dominant dyad vis-à-vis family leadership rather than the U.S. notion of the husband-wife team is not atypical in many parts of Latin America (Falicov 1988b); it may be played out in this particular manner given the Guatemalan historical context.

Second, women may be more pressed to take the initiative to migrate nowadays as wartime psychology means the loss of Guatemalan men to terrorism and violence in greater numbers than the women. I talked to one Indian woman who was traveling through the Bay Area sponsored by a church group. Her contention was that the Indian and Ladina women were forced to take on a stronger role in the family because of the ever present involvement of the men in the civil conflict. Of course, this phenomenon can be seen much more dramatically in the Indian refugee camps than among urban Ladino migrants.

Finally, once they are in the United States, women can easily find work as domestics. Men have a more difficult time, and the nature of the work they are involved in—restaurant, factory, construction, farm labor, and so forth—is somewhat less clandestine. While the earnings of the men may be greater (and they may not be), there are many dangers in finding and holding jobs. Men do not find supportive patrons as easily as do their wives, who may develop close dependency relationships with their employers. This situation creates a strain for marital relationships in which Guatemalan men expect to be the primary wage-earner, supporter, and family protector.

The process of coping with the new U.S. environment is a minefield of dangers for immigrant Guatemalan families. Marital relationships become sorely tested. Women find that very private decisions such as marriage become socially influenced. Marrying someone with the legal documents to live in the United States can mean a lot, not only for the woman but for her children as well. One woman in this study (Olga Menchú-Franzi) managed to bring her children into the United States this way. Perhaps because of these opportunities, Guatemalan women tend to attach loyalty first to family and then to country; they also develop substitute attachments in the United States more quickly than do the Guatemalan men. The historical role of the Guatemalan woman has been to serve as a buffer between the dominant Spanish-European society and the dominated Indian native tradition. The Guatemalan immigrant woman continues this role in the United States. The social, sexual, and economic mores in the United States set the stage for the Guatemalan woman to mediate between the native culture left behind and the new American future. As is true in race relations generally, Latin American women are perceived as less of a threat to the dominant society than the men. Guatemalan men have less to gain in the United States than Guatemalan women; they may be resentful and envious of the greater options available to their wives. Socially and economically as well as psychologically, it is also more difficult for them to find American wives in the same way that Guatemalan women find American husbands.

Reunification is another crucial factor in straining family relations. Most immigrant families have existed in fragmented form for a number of years prior to the reestablishment of the family living together in the United States. In many cases the family has never lived in the same household, or there are family members who have never met each other before. Family members, particularly adolescents (but also husbands and wives), are accustomed to living under different sets of rules, often entirely independently. Suddenly everyone feels restricted and tension is inevitable, conflict likely.

Drinking behavior is one indicator of how well families are doing in the United States. Gordon (1978) reports that drinking behavior decreased following the migration of Dominican families to the New Jersey area. He attributes increased sobriety to the economic improvement (also see Graves 1967) and social pressure of the extended family and community in the new setting. In the case of the Guatemalan families in this study, at least two of the fathers encountered trouble with reversion to problem drinking. Gordon's thesis is valid for his sample, but the families in this study are not finding the economic improvement and advancement that they had hoped for in the United States. The depressed economic state of affairs generally found in the 1980s and now in the 1990s has not created much room for hope for these men. At the same time, the U.S. public, political and governmental figures, and the media are giving much attention to the "immigration problem." Contemporary acculturation studies are reporting more stress-related illness for acculturating groups, but they have not focused on what it is like to attempt to adapt in a xenophobic, hostile environment.

Marital conflict is the process of bringing the Guatemalan civil war to a new front, the home front, in a new setting. Women are struggling to adapt quickly, look to the future, and see that future in their children. Men maintain their loyalty to past traditions, develop techniques of symbolically returning to Guatemala, and reject a future in the United States that offers them less than it provides their wives. They also see their future in their children, but they see that future as back in Guatemala.

How does this type of marital civil war affect the family as a whole? What does the uprooting, migration, and resettlement experience mean for the adolescent in the family?

The 1980s and 1990s are decades of preparation for all youth, not just for Guatemalan immigrants. The increased rate of suicide among U.S. adolescents as well as child abuse and incest have received much media attention. The demographic shift in the United States is to the older generation—the baby boomers who have grown up. Never has it been less of a privilege to be young in the United States (Spencer 1979). But the adolescents in these Guatemalan families have made the pilgrimage not only because of the violence at home in Guatemala but because their families had some hope that things would be better here. Often, their families have sacrificed a good deal to bring them to the United States.

Outwardly the youth in the families in this study appear strong. They are polite and gracious, mature and open to learn. They articulate clear ideas as to what they want for their futures. They do not manifest the sense of adolescent moratorium, rebellion, or malaise that is often common with U.S. teenagers, or even with second or third generation immigrant youth. Generally, they scoff at American punk, Chicano *cholo*, or other adolescent subcultures. In one high school they voted overwhelmingly to adopt conservative-looking school uniforms.

But just beneath the surface, most of the adolescents are riddled with insecurities and innumerable worries and fears. Their futures are clearly in question. In five out of six of the families, the adolescent children are currently ineligible for college education or any training program in the United States after they complete high school because of their illegal immigration status. They are dependent on the good will of relatives with residency or on future developments in U.S. educational and immigration policy and law. The youth in this study are so tense that most have insomnia and at least three report persistent difficulty with loss of appetite and stomach aches, which are indicators of depression and anxiety. They report nightmares of falling, jumping off a cliff, being chased, killed, and so forth. Another common theme is that they have to put on an act for others, act like a "dummy," perform, and get stared at. Their dreams reflect the pressures they are feeling and the resultant sense of living in a fishbowl. They are suffering from cultural paranoia, from trying to live up to so many expectations. Being Guatemalans, they are a clear minority, even among Latinos, so they feel even more isolated.

The dreams of parents in these families are generally less dramatic than those of the teenagers, but they too have the theme of following a goal such as making money in the United States. In the parents' dreams, however, they often lose their way, find that the money is worthless, and discover that their dream was in vain. They dream mainly of Guatemala, and there is a nostalgic quality to the reports. Parents are expressing symbolic repatriation while their children dream of the United States and are full of the fears of a lost identity and a questionable future.

NEW DIRECTIONS IN MIGRANT MENTAL HEALTH

This study offers a particular perspective on uprooted Guatemalans that bears on theories of migration and family life and the application of these theories to mental health. There are four principal theoretical and practical contributions made in this research: (1) use of the nuclear family as the unit of study of a larger phenomenon; (2) sensitivity to the nuances of change and adaptation as processes rather than as types or outcomes; (3) convergence of historical-structural and acculturational orientations; and (4) concern for the dynamics of cultural constancy following migration.

First, use of the family as the unit of analysis in this study is significant in that it establishes the family as a useful conceptual tool for studying a wide range of larger-scale social phenomena (urbanization, fertility patterns, epidemiology, gerontology, educational systems, and occupational structures, to name a few examples). The family is especially important for the survival of Guatemalan immigrants and refugees, and attention to the family system is a necessity for human service practioners. The father is often particularly vulnerable, having to cope with downward social mobility and role reversal with his newly empowered wife. The expectations placed on the adolescent in the Guatemalan family system are often enormous and unrealistic. Although there are clear differences in perception and experience of its members, family interdependence is maintained through the women who are the initiators of migration, the buffers with the hostile environment, and the moral leaders of the household. Teachers, doctors, employers, counselors, therapists, legislators, and human service administrators are advised to consider the impact of their interventions and policies on these families, and to look for ways to enhance the roles and coping strategies of the diverse family members.

A second area in which this study relates to theory and practice is in its emphasis on process and development in examining migrant motives, psychological adjustment, and family mental health. There is a common pitfall in migration theory—that of dealing with the phenomenon as a unit that can be divided into exclusive categories and subcategories: types and outcomes. I choose to emphasize this concern even though I am well aware that it comes at a time when outcome measures are of great moment and immigration policies are becoming more restrictive to new arrivals. Such analysis is flawed, however, in that it is limited to a cross-sectional slice in time. It essentially ignores the significance of the broader context such as demographic trends, international political and economic policies, and social and cultural history, as well as important biographical data of the migrants themselves. It is far better to examine the processes of change that take place following migration longitudinally and in stages. This means that the results of my study are not written in concrete. Instead, they describe strategies and processes that are subject to alteration as outside demands, life cycle and personal needs, and perspectives change—and as people learn from their experience. The notion of process and development also instills some hope for future change.

There is another, more ominous element to the notion of process versus types and outcomes. It is the dialectic between the host society (in this case, the United States), the sending society (Guatemala), and the people who are voting with their feet. The narrative format used in this book is designed to give these immigrants flesh and bones as three-dimensional people rather than as depersonalized research subjects. It would be a disservice to them to see them only as types or outcomes, since they are so often devalued by the public at large and, when not needed for menial labor, are deported by U.S. authorities. Such humanization makes it more difficult to use simple ideological justifications for U.S. foreign policy decisions. It is also not as easy to insist on strict western diagnostic criteria for humanitarian treatment of what Victor Perera calls the *mala saña* or the "fury. . . rage in the marrow," that infects many refugees of a war that is hidden from much of the world (Perera 1986, p. 184).

Third, the point of view taken in this study is that each theoretical approach to migration—historical-structural and acculturational/phenomenological—leans on the other in serving to correct what the other approach lacks. Accordingly, I have avoided relying on either approach exclusively; instead, I have taken a simultaneous tri-level approach that derives from and weds both views. In this convergence, the most personal reasons for choosing to come to the United States are shaped and influenced by conditions and events. Although serendipity and chance are undoubtedly factors as well, it seems that personal and family crises tend to occur when people need the courage or the spark to push or pull them over the edge of a decision.

Building on this convergence, it can be seen that coping and adaptation take place in a host community that is becoming demoralized in the 1990s with an economic downturn that affects the lower stratum of society especially harshly. Guatemalan immigrants coming into this situation are impacted by negative community reaction to their dreams and energy; they are often perceived not as the resourceful people and contributors they are but as threats to "a piece of the pie." Those who are refugees may still be reeling from survivors' guilt and the "subversive identity" conferred upon them by the Guatemalan government. Simple definitions of post-traumatic stress may not do justice to the fact that the injuries inflicted on the new arrivals have been and are continuing to be produced socially, by groups, organizations, governments, institutions, and by random violence. The Jesuit priest and Salvadoran social psychologist Ignacio Martin-Baró wrote brilliantly about this situation before he was assassinated. His pleas to Central American countries and the United States were to "depolarize, deideologize, and demilitarize" (Martin-Baró 1988, p. 12).

The fourth area and most relevant contribution to anthropological, migration, and family theory is that of cultural constancy. This study provides evidence of the continuity, even centripetality, in how Guatemalan culture is maintained in families even after they have moved to another cultural milieu. In this early stage, at least, the Spanish language is dominant and there are material symbols of national or cultural loyalty. The Guatemalan national identity that is at once hidden, cautious, and restrained, as well as proud, strong, and resilient, is also still found. The families, too, share goals of future achievement and a moral-religious quest for meaning in their new lives. In concentrating on future educational and economic goals, they focus on the children and on keeping the family together. Religious involvement, with both evangelical and Catholic churches, turns out to be an important aspect of cultural constancy for these families. Finding culturally congruent ways of healing (*deshecharse,*[8] rituals, etc.) is especially important. Many have been traumatized directly, many more indirectly. They have all suffered significant losses and separations. Most feel their families are disunited. The Spanish-speaking evangelical churches give the disunited families spiritual and ideological guidelines. Migrants look to these churches for healing, spiritual and emotional support, contact with other Latinos, and familiar Guatemalan norms and values.

Cultural constancy is subject to massive centrifugal forces as well. First, the stresses of settling into new homes, finding housing and employment, and coping with undocumented status are severe. Parents give up goals such as satisfying work for themselves and home ownership so that their families can be together and their children can have a chance to get an education and a job in the United States. They tolerate assaults on their dignity, take risks in making expensive clandestine overland journeys with only the aid of strangers, and are forced to open themselves to an entirely new set of values and customs in the United States. Add to this the normal adolescent conflicts over autonomy, and cultural and family loyalties become strained sometimes to the breaking point.

There are also centrifugal forces within the Guatemalan culture itself deriving from conflicts that have existed throughout Guatemalan history and that have never been resolved. The family cultures in the case studies reflect these consistent themes in the Guatemalan historical panorama. Families are caught up in the ancient split between Indian and Hispanic identities. What hopes they might have had for the resolution of this and other schisms were dashed in 1954 with the return of the police state. These families now flee 4,000 miles from home, but they bring the gnawing contradictions with them. Historical conflicts between men and women, Indians and Ladinos, as well as modern-day conflicts between leftists and rightists, Catholics and evangelicals, and Guatemalan nationalists and U.S. assimilationists are subjects that arouse intense but (usually) covert power struggles within families. The family themes or cultural styles reflect the sense of poignant civil struggle for integration of cultural identity at the most intimate family level: success, conflict, adventure, freedom, sacrifice, death, nationalism, solidarity, and obligation.

The theoretical significance of cultural constancy can be found in the dynamic centripetal and centrifugal processes that alter and maintain the culture following migration. With the families themselves, the theme of family separation and its counterpart, reunification, emerges repeatedly. The tension and conflict found in these families are also likely accompaniments to family reunification after prolonged separation. In spite of the pain, conflict serves a positive function for the families as a whole and for individual members. The act of migrating and reconstituting family and household is an attempt to resolve differences and cultural dichotomies. Through migration, these families opt for creating a crisis of possibilities in which growth and resolution can take place.

The process of family integration can be seen most directly in the role of the adolescents. The youth work diligently to live up to their parents' hopes and dreams, even though privately they remain insecure and fearful, facing formidable obstacles in reaching these high goals. Collectively, they know they are symbols of achievement and identity integration for the entire family.

The tenacity of these Guatemalan families in surviving the tragedies and trials that they have endured in their odysseys to the United States is something that therapists, teachers, health practitioners, and policymakers should not take lightly. In their dreams at night, family members face up to each other. Their heroes and heroines are members of their own families. But there is psychological baggage that accompanies endurance. Most members of study families report a good deal of dissatisfaction with their family life. Schisms are still painfully evident, and it is a lot to expect that the adolescent or the church can resolve them. While these families show obvious strengths and assets, closer scrutiny reveals the ghosts that still disturb their sleep.

Theoreticians and practitioners alike would do well to reject ethnocentric approaches and to look more closely at the origin societies of migrant groups.   This study has sought to view migration and resettlement as a process of discovery. The experience of discovery is exhausting in that it has taken months and even years for these families to resettle together under one roof.   Through reunification, the six families in the study are changing in response to the demands placed upon them by their new home in the United States.   But at the same time, the roles the family members take with each other and the faces they show to the outside world reflect a clouded mirror that goes back 400 years and 4,000 miles.

EPILOGUE

What is to become of Gordon, the fresh-faced, sad-eyed miracle student? Is this a possible scenario?

It is three years later, winter in San Francisco. A wind-swept rain washes the streets. Gordon is overjoyed. He runs home leaping over puddles, jacket open, oblivious to the rain. The school counselor had good news for him; he's been accepted into an agronomy program at the university. Everything is falling into place. His brother returned suddenly to Guatemala a year ago, bequeathing him a forged residency card as a parting gift. He and his mother have been saving money—and the counselor says he qualifies for a partial fellowship. He can hardly wait to tell his mother. Flinging open the door, he hears the telephone ringing. It is his uncle in Guatemala. His brother has been shot and is in a hospital in Guatemala City. "We cannot give details over the telephone." They need money desperately for medical expenses. Of course. Gordon feels light-headed; there is a flash of the nightmare image of the cliff and the crowd, the sense of entrapment. There is a dull ache in the pit of his stomach. But he keeps on talking to his uncle while his mother screams and cries.

Appendix 1

MINI-ETHNOGRAPHY OF THE GUATEMALAN-AMERICAN IMMIGRANT COMMUNITY IN THE SAN FRANCISCO BAY AREA

The fieldwork for this study was accomplished from October 1982 through March 1984. Early in the fieldwork period, I traveled briefly (for two weeks in December 1982) to Mexico and Guatemala with my husband and children in order to gather more background information on home conditions that may be precipitating migration. It had been twelve years since I had been to Guatemala, and I also needed to update my knowledge of the current conditions. On this trip I visited with family members—my uncle, aunt, and three cousins who are currently exiles in Mexico. In getting their perspectives, I was able to broaden my understanding of the situation for immigrant families in the United States as well as my own place in the contemporary scene.

Back in the United States, I developed a data collection process for the purpose of preparing a small urban ethnography of Guatemalan immigration patterns. I made approximately ninety-two contacts with key informants using an unstructured interview format.

The largest category of contacts (31) was school personnel. Actually, these individuals were key to my access to the study population, the Guatemalan teenagers themselves and their families. Because of their critical role with the adolescents, I needed to spend a good deal of time with them.

The second largest group of contacts (29) was Guatemalan migrants who did not fit into the strictures of my formal research design (i.e., they had not been here for less than three years with teenage children) or who did not complete the series of interviews following the interview schedules.

Next, I talked with ten persons who could be loosely termed as "key individuals" unaffiliated with institutions. They were involved in networks associated with Guatemalan migrant families. The rest of my informants were affiliated with other organizations and institutions relating to Central American immigrants. Nine were health clinic personnel; six were staff members of various refugee aid organizations; five were church personnel; and five were involved in the arts and/or political affinity groups. A number of the latter were mostly concerned with Indian refugees in Mexico.

RECONNAISSANCE IN GUATEMALA

Immersion in the fieldwork process seemed to be only one-sided for me until, as part of a migrating family system myself, I decided to visit Guatemala. My husband and two daughters (ages 4 and 9) accompanied me.

On our arrival in Guatemala City on December 16, 1982, the atmosphere seemed noticeably less cosmopolitan and frantic than in Mexico City, which we had just left. The airport was breezy and easy to maneuver, small and with considerably less military presence than I had anticipated. However, we did have to fill out a customs slip indicating if we had brought any communications equipment into Guatemala (such as tape recorders) and for what purpose they were intended. We also saw and heard a number of military helicopters flying around. As we approached the center of Guatemala City, we scanned a sea of green khaki camouflage uniforms; a more pronounced army presence suddenly seemed to be everywhere. The machine guns were not slung over the soldiers' shoulders but, rather, were held in both hands, at rest, but ready. Faces were impassive and eyes were constantly moving. The soldiers were young, early teenagers, predominantly dark, Indian. They made no eye contact with the populace. Guatemala City was very congested with many more Indians and campesinos selling their wares on the streets than I remembered from my visit twelve years before. I imagined that many had migrated to the capital from the rural areas due to economic upheaval and violence.

When we arrived, we checked in at the U.S. Embassy and ended up speaking briefly with the U.S. consul, Phillip Taylor. He laughingly said that things were very calm but that we should be careful on the buses. Two buses had been burned the day before due to anger among the citizenry over an increase of five to ten cents in the fare. He said he couldn't suggest that it was safe to drive on the highways at night or to drive toward Lake Atitlán or Chichicastenango because "If you're in a lightning storm, you don't climb up the tree where you're an easier target for the lightening."

During our visit we had intended to visit three people: the director of the National Indian Institute (whom we had met on our previous trip); a family friend (a seventy-year old woman who had been a close friend of my grandmother); and the uncle of a Guatemalan family living in the United States whom I had begun to interview as part of my study population. I was unable to locate the Indian Institute in the telephone book. I spoke to the curator of the Museo Popol Vuh but she did not know of its existence or of José Castañeda, its director. The place seemed to have vanished into thin air. I had heard about massacres a few years back at Indian centers in Guatemala City. Perhaps the National Indian Institute was a casualty of the terrorism and upheaval that seemed to characterize Guatemala at this time. The family friend whom we called seemed unwilling to let us call on her at her home. Instead, she came to meet us at our hotel along with another woman friend of hers. Both of them were dressed in stylish pastel suits; they visited with us briefly in the hotel lobby, engaging in small talk. One of their social group (of elderly women) was ill in the hospital and they were off to visit her. They seemed reluctant to talk with us as I had hoped; instead, they seemed nervous and rushed. Just as we were despairing of making any good contacts with Guatemalans, we reached Dr. Valencia (a pseudonym) by telephone, the relative of a family in the study that had migrated to the United States recently. He lived in the neighboring city of Antigua, to which we had planned to travel.

We drove to Antigua two days after our arrival in Guatemala City. Before we left, we took a last look at downtown Guatemala City. The dust and exhaust fumes were stirred by the windy weather, and traffic and congestion were very thick. There seemed to be more crowding than I remembered from twelve years ago, that is, until we reached the city center, the National Palace. The Palace faces a large square park that was almost deserted. There was no parking on any street near the Palace. There was a line of soldiers in front of the Palace, about twenty to twenty-five of them. As we approached, we realized that we were the only people on the street. Here we were, a man, woman, and two little girls, walking in front of the Palace, a barred iron gate at the entrance with a large armored car facing the street behind it. The soldiers backed up as we approached, machine gun butts poking through the foliage. I realized that we were no longer visiting the National Palace, but rather a military garrison. We needed no more encouragement to head out for Antigua.

Upon arrival, we visited the home of Dr. Valencia. He introduced me to his wife and two of his young sons. He lived in a beautiful home with an Indian servant working in the kitchen. He showed me around and pointed out the extensive remodeling that had been done after the 1976 earthquake. In our conversation, he said it was quite true that many people were leaving Guatemala. He said that families were breaking up, that among his extended family, individuals have gone little by little to different parts of the United States. A sister of his moved to New Orleans and married an American; when she comes to visit him in Guatemala, she and her husband speak only English. His other sister went to live with her daughter and son-in-law in the San Francisco Bay Area. Those who leave Guatemala emigrate for economic reasons, because of the violence, and for personal reasons as well. Dr. Valencia anticipated that the conflict would last another three to five years. As a physician, he noted that the medical problems he was now treating included more ulcers, arthritis, gastritis, anxiety neurosis, and depression. He saw it as clearly connected to the break-up of families and the disappearances of family members. He did not think that those who left for the United States would ever return. He said that three of his sons were training to be doctors. One had been forced by the government as part of the internship program to go to work in an *aldea* (small village) where there was much violence. If he hadn't gone, he would have been jailed. The whole family had been very worried about him, but he came out all right. Throughout the interview, Dr. Valencia coughed persistently and spoke in a flat tone of voice, without animation; he appeared to be depressed himself.

We spent most of the rest of our visit in Antigua, the pride of Guatemala, an elegant small city full of majestic ruins and churches. Antigua was the ecclesiastical heart of Central America for four centuries and the colonial capital as well. There was little evidence of the massacres taking place in the highlands. However, in the plaza, soldiers perched on top of a ruined wall, semi-hiding in the shadows, always with the same machine guns. A waiter in our hotel in Antigua engaged us in conversation about how difficult life has been in Guatemala "since the earthquake." When I asked him about people leaving the country, he stated emphatically that those who leave are cowards and do not have the perseverance to stay and try to rebuild the country. The same evening, however, a bartender inquired of my husband where he was from in California. When he heard San Francisco, he asked my husband if he could come to work for him on his *finca* (ranch) in San Francisco, picking grapes and apples!

When we returned to Guatemala City in preparation for the trip home, we found the capital more tense, with military guards at our hotel and in the parking lot. An incident had occurred a few days previously:

The daughter of the president of Honduras, Dr. Judith Xiomara Suazo (who was a physician at a Guatemala City hospital) had been kidnapped by a new guerrilla organization with the stipulation that she would be released if the government broadcast a message from the guerrilla organization. The government had until Friday, this date, to accomplish this; otherwise she would be killed. Throughout the week, Ríos Montt had flip-flopped on what he would do, saying at first that he would not accede to any of the kidnappers' demands. Accompanying this statement was the message that a vigorous house-to-house search was being conducted in Guatemala City. This was in the newspapers. On our way driving back into Guatemala City on this final day of the deadline, we saw an army truck filled with soldiers that had stopped a municipal bus loaded with campesinos. All had been forced to disembark, and their knapsacks and huge bags and packages were being searched. At the same time, on the car radio we began hearing the message of the guerrilla organization being broadcast. When we reached our hotel we also heard it several times on the television, and it was in the newspapers. That evening, the broadcast of the guerrilla manifesto was followed by an interview with the distraught aunt of the kidnap victim: She read a letter pleading for the life of her niece. Then came an announcement from an organization of media professionals stating that they were no longer going to broadcast these types of manifestos.

Throughout the week, indications were that the media were quite censored and controlled. Actual news coverage was minimal, sensationalistic, and lacking in-depth analysis. On an earlier day, our children were watching American cartoons on television (dubbed in Spanish) when a "public service program" suddenly appeared on the screen teaching people how to deal with "home accidents." Soft, lilting music came on in the background, and a woman with a soothing voice appeared to demonstrate how to care for injuries such as what looked like second or third degree burns as a result of that occasional "home accident." This came complete with graphic illustrations on the screen. When we changed the channel, we discovered that the message (with all its subliminal overlay) was being broadcast on every channel and on every radio station as well.

The next day we caught our flight out of Guatemala City. When we arrived home, we read that Dr. Judith Xiomara Suazo had been released unharmed. In speaking with Dr. Valencia's relatives in the Bay Area, I found that Dr. Valencia had written to them after we left to inform them that he wanted to come to the United States. He asked them to help him locate a job.

THE BAY AREA GUATEMALAN NETWORK

The heart of this study is the work that was done with six Guatemalan immigrant families. However, as an adjunct to the family studies, I also explored the Bay Area Guatemalan network. This process actually served two purposes: (1) to develop a small ethnography, and (2) to indirectly select some of the families who would be in my study population. Some of the informants I interviewed were known to me as friends and acquaintances before I began this research. Others were suggested to me when I telephoned schools, health clinics, churches, and immigrant and refugee aid organizations. Many of these individuals knew and worked with each other and referred people to each other. Others worked in isolation and had little to do with the loosely tied networks.

The material gathered through this process can be divided into four main topics: (1) Guatemalan and Central American demographic data; (2) how Guatemalans get here: (3) motives and meaning of the Guatemalan migration; and (4) cultural identity and the Guatemalan family and adolescent in the United States.

Guatemalan and Central American Demographic Data

There are no good demographic data on Central American refugee-ism and migration at the present time. This is because most of the movement of people is clandestine and illegal. Catholic church sources (Ferguson, D. 1984) have estimated that besides the internal displacement that has taken place in the various Central American countries, about 12 percent of the populations have fled to another country. Most immigrants and refugees have not fled far—they have merely crossed one border, staying with extended family or friends if possible, or have ended up in refugee camps in Mexico, Honduras, Nicaragua, and Costa Rica. Of the estimated (again by Catholic sources—Ferguson, D. 1984) 350,000 to 500,000 Central Americans who have come to the United States from 1980 to 1985, about one-sixth or one-seventh have chosen the San Francisco Bay area as their home. These figures may underestimate the number of Central American expatriates, and they do not include those who have come since 1985. It could be a life-and-death matter to identify oneself as coming from a Central American country, particularly from El Salvador or Guatemala. For this reason, many who come to the United States illegally may be passing themselves off as Mexican; being deported to Mexico is not life-threatening, and there is only one border to cross in order to return.

The San Francisco Bay Area is well known as a magnet for Central Americans in the United States. It is one of only two U.S. urban areas in which Central Americans predominate among the Latinos. (The other is Washington, D.C.). Central American dominance continues to grow in this area as the refugees keep pouring in.

Nicaraguans have historically been the largest group of Central Americans in the San Francisco area. Recent waves have consisted of the anti-Somocistas (those opposed to the Somoza family dictatorship), young professionals, and the anti-Sandinistas (those who lost positions and property in the 1978 revolution). Since the Sandinistas lost control of the government, there has not been a noticeable return migration of Bay Area Nicaraguans.

In comparison, the Salvadoran refugee population has skyrocketed. The Salvadoran community in the Bay Area has doubled since 1980 from 60,000–70,000 to 100,000–150,000 in 1984. Most of the new arrivals have come since 1981. (Figures are from the Catholic Archdiocese of San Francisco.) These are generally people who are fleeing violence and a collapsed economy. As such they represent the socioeconomic spectrum, with working- and lower-middle-class people, especially young men (ages 15-30), predominating. Until recently, official Immigration and Naturalization Service figures put Guatemalan and Salvadoran immigration at about the same numbers nationwide. These figures are notoriously inadequate (they are out of date, and they count only legal as opposed to all immigrants). Bay Area sources estimate that the majority of the new immigrants from Latin America are Salvadoran; second are Mexicans with Nicaraguans and Guatemalans tied for third. In San Francisco, at any rate, Salvadorans have become the most populous Latin American immigrant group.

Guatemala is third on the list of Central American countries with a strong host population in the San Francisco Bay Area. Closer geographically to the United States than El Salvador, Guatemala has developed ties with the United States over the last half century (United Fruit Company, Del Monte, tourism, etc.) During the Arbenz and Arévalo socialist administrations in Guatemala (1944–1954), U.S.-Guatemala relations cooled considerably. At that time, visas to travel in the United States were infrequently granted to Guatemalans. Later, in the 1950s and 1960s after the U.S.-sponsored coup, middle-class Guatemalans began emigrating to the United States. In the 1960s, direct air flights to San Francisco were initiated, encouraging continued emigration. In general, these cohorts constitute the host Guatemalan-American community today. This community has a more middle- to upper-class reputation in comparison to other Latino communities in the Bay Area. It is not considered to be typical of Central Americans but only of a certain elite upper socioeconomic stratum.

In the early 1970s, Guatemala's population explosion and economic crunch led to widespread discontent among the campesino, Indian, and professional classes. Peasants from the countryside moved to towns and, ultimately, to Guatemala City, often shedding Indian clothes and identities. By 1981, in certain parts of Guatemala the upheaval took on the character of war; many Indians and Ladinos became internal refugees, and the Mexican border swelled with 50,000 Indian refugees.

As a consequence of these events, there has been an increase in Guatemalan immigrants and refugees coming into the San Francisco Bay Area since 1980. It is almost impossible to estimate how big the increase has been; but it certainly does not approach that of the Salvadoran influx. Compared to the Salvadorans, Guatemalans seem to have more family connections here. One informant working at an English language school in San Francisco's Mission district told me that Guatemalans now constitute 10 percent of her students. The percentage has doubled in two years, she noted. Other informants corroborated a slight increase in Guatemalans, and they see more working- and lower-middle-class Ladinos than before when the middle classes predominated. This new stream of migrants in the Bay Area is composed of more young single individuals, mostly urban males. There are also a large number of young professionals, students, teachers, church workers, medical personnel, and so forth.

Although the San Francisco Bay Area is a popular destination for Central American emigrants, a number of other places are also chosen. Mexico is probably the most common destination for Guatemalan and Salvadoran immigrants. Mexico has historically served as a refuge for the politically oppressed in Latin America because of linguistic/cultural affinities and geographic proximity. Some Guatemalans, particularly members of the political left, go to Canada—especially Toronto and Montreal—since these communities played host to Arbenz and his supporters when he was overthrown in 1954. There are even some exiles in Australia. Other U.S. cities attracting large numbers of Central Americans are Chicago; Washington, D.C.; Miami; and New York City. Many campesino migrants gravitate to (or get stuck in) migrant labor camps in Texas or in California, working the vineyards of the Salinas Valley north to Napa and beyond.

Within the United States, the overwhelmingly most popular destination is Los Angeles. The Central American population there is probably two or three times that of the Bay Area. Again, Salvadorans constitute the majority of the Central Americans there (300,000 in 1984), but there is also a sizeable Guatemalan community (100,000 in 1984). There are some communities in the downtown area in which entire Central American villages have been transplanted. Los Angeles immigrants from Latin American countries have a more proletarian reputation than do those of the San Francisco Bay Area. Among Guatemalan refugees and migrants, there are groups of Indians and one Mam-speaking community in Westgate. Families with women workers are also attracted to the large garment industry there (Peñalosa 1986).

The San Francisco Bay Area is not as spread out as the Los Angeles region; it boasts better transportation and services, as well as a more familiar Central American ambience in the Mission district. As a destination, it is often the result of a secondary move from Los Angeles. Factory work may be found across the San Francisco Bay in the East Bay region. Guatemalan-Americans with money or a strong upwardly mobile bent sometimes move to the San Mateo peninsula of bedroom communities adjacent to San Francisco. San Mateo and Burlingame, especially, are known for their expatriate, politically conservative, Guatemalan-American population. Not the least of the attractions of the Bay Area for Guatemalans and other Central Americans is that there is less raiding by the immigration police, *la migra,* in comparison to what is experienced in Los Angeles. All of these attractions are being eroded as the current stalled economy of the 1990s is taking its toll on services, transportation, available work and the tolerance of the host economy for immigrants.

How Guatemalans Get Here

Guatemalans enter the United States in three ways: (1) through legal immigration, usually through petition by a relative, a parent, or a sibling; (2) by applying for a visa; and (3) overland, or *mojado.* The first method takes several years, so it is really only of long-term value, not a step to be taken if action must be immediate. The only other legal recourse, political asylum, is still extremely difficult for Central Americans to obtain at this time.

The second method, application for a visa, is also difficult to accomplish. It requires some sophistication in dealing with the U.S. Embassy and a large amount of money. Applicants must demonstrate that they have financial investments that would bring them home; and they must present a round-trip ticket costing around $1,000.[1] It also probably helps to know someone inside the Embassy. Even so, applications are often rejected. A Guatemalan official at the U.S. Embassy in Guatemala City told me that about half of the requests for visas are turned down. He said that about 40 percent of those entering the United States on a tourist visa (the most common way) do not return. Embassy officials are often quite arbitrary as to whom they grant the visas to and to whom they don't, he added.

The third method of entry is overland, *indocumentado* (undocumented and/or without legal status or "papers") or *mojado*. Although in the past Guatemalans have enjoyed the reputation in the Latin community of being the most "legal" of the Central American immigrants, this may no longer be true. A number of informants told me that most Guatemalans were middle class and had visas, wealthy patrons, and resources here in the United States; but when it came down to actual cases and trends, it appeared that these were only a visible minority of the Guatemalan migrants. The majority of the new arrivals are probably as *mojado* as the Salvadoran refugees.

Those who are *mojado* are typically poorer or working class. Ads in the newspaper in Guatemala for *excursiones a los estados unidos* (U.S. tours) are codes for *coyotes* (or guides) for the novice to cross into the United States. These individuals usually take people in groups upon payment of a lump sum, usually $800 to $1,000 quetzales (equivalent to the same number of U.S. dollars) per head. This can amount to quite a large sum of money for a large family. Individuals may borrow from friends, relatives, compadres, or loan sharks. Sometimes people are under duress to make decisions quickly as to who will go and how they will make the trip. Then furniture or valuables may be pawned, the house may be mortgaged, and all money in the bank may be withdrawn to finance the trip for certain family members. Others may have to find cheaper methods—walking, sneaking onto buses or freight transport, stealing, and so forth. In such cases, the journey to the United States may take months. They may need to stop along the way to work to raise the capital for the next leg of the journey. Those who are brought in by *coyotes* stay in homes or hotels that make a business of sheltering *mojados*.

The journey is a perilous one, *coyote* notwithstanding. The travelers are innocents abroad. They are so vulnerable to anyone taking advantage of them that they are often victimized. Horror stories abound of people being killed, robbed, charged double for services, raped, and even captured and put into slavery. They have, of course, no recourse or redress for any of these crimes or indignities. One informant told me that the best advice was to find a *coyote* in church.

The most difficult part of the journey is the crossing of the U.S.-Mex-

ico border. Those taking buses are often caught at the checkpoint
Benjamin Hill in Mexico near the U.S. border. Women are sometimes
raped there. A $10 bribe may allow the traveler to pass. Most
individuals cross the border at Tijuana, El Paso, Nogales, Mexicali, or a
number of other border towns. Many get false crossing permits through
bribery; others must sneak across when immigration officials are not
looking. Guatemalans (and Salvadorans) lack experience with the border
subculture. Since they are strangers in Mexico and are unfamiliar with
the geographical, social, and cultural terrain, they are easy targets for
official governmental agents and independent operators on both sides of
the border. Guatemalan Spanish is also notably different from Mexican
Spanish, so Guatemalan *mojados* may be detected by their language
patterns.

The trip from the border to Los Angeles is generally made at night.
It is said to be the most harrowing and frightening part of the trip. Once
in Los Angeles, however, contacts are made with family, friends, or
cheros (superficial, casual acquaintances, usually peers).   Unlucky
travelers may have to sleep in bus stations, abandoned cars, parks, and
similar places. Often, help can be found through church organizations.

Families come up in chain migration fashion. Among the middle-class
families, husbands ordinarily enter first. They attempt to save enough
money to send for their wives and children. Probably a more common
pattern is for (1) poorer women who are heads of household to bring up
their families singlehandedly, and (2) young males, ages 15 to 30 to
wander northward in a less purposeful fashion. Many of these traveling
youths do not have close ties to their families of origin and are striking
out on their own. Sometimes they come to stay with distant relatives
whom they have never met; tensions and clashes may develop soon
afterward. The relatives may evict them, and they become wanderers,
bewildered and confused.

Motives and Meaning of the Guatemalan Migration

There are two major streams of Guatemalan immigrants and refugees
at this time: working-class migrants and middle-class refugees. There
is also another group of sojourners who are not really migrants, but
rather visitors; these are the wealthy and the elite classes.

The largest group is that of the poor and working-class peoples.
Laborers and tradesmen make the journey because they are pushed out
by massive unemployment and underemployment. They come because
they have connections here, because they can no longer support their

families at home, or because their families have disintegrated. Informants stressed to me the effect of the high inflation rate and low salaries
(averaging 30 to 75 quetzales a month) on the emigration rate over the
past few years. They told me that many peasants in the countryside are
starving; many fear for their lives. Once they have made the move to
Guatemala City, they find that they still cannot survive as petty vendors,
hawking little trinkets and shining shoes on street corners. Some are
reduced to thievery; others come north.

Once they have arrived, they are compelled to take any kind of work
so that they can send remittances home. Many utilize church connections (especially in the evangelical churches) to find odd jobs; others find
service occupations in upscale elite homes and restaurants. They
develop an urbane polish and vocabulary. The youth and the females
have an easier time finding work and adapting. Those who are less
successful economically suffer from depression, anxiety, and a loss of
self-worth. Extended setbacks often lead to excessive drinking among
Guatemalan men and other forms of self-defeating behavior.

The wealthy classes in Guatemala are those of independent means.
They live on business investments, family connections, and government
jobs. One informant summed it up as *cuello,* or "pull." People with
cuello still do fairly well in Guatemala; most informants felt that they had
no reason to leave. Those with *cuello* can get visas easily, and because
of ready access to money, they travel back and forth to the United States
with ease. The traveling is mainly to Miami where many businessmen
keep their assets. Others have family connections in the San Francisco
Bay Area. For the "comfortable," this situation has existed for several
decades. These days, however, some are using their connections to come
for reasons other than business and family visiting. Young men,
especially, often come out of fear of being kidnapped and robbed by
guerilleros. Some have been threatened; a nephew of one of my
informants was kidnapped and robbed by *guerilleros*, so he came to live
in the Bay Area for a time with relatives. Studying at Guatemala's
prestigious University of San Carlos can be very dangerous nowadays, so
some college-age students of means come here to study. Generally,
however, the wealthy classes or those with *cuello* in Guatemala do not
adapt well to life in the United States. They do not have the privileges
that they have at home; they miss the social life of visiting and parties.
They find that they do not have the leisure time afforded to them back
home with servants to make life more comfortable. They dislike the
impersonal, legalistic form of relationships that exists here. If they can,
they return home.

The second major stream of Guatemalan immigrants, then, is not the wealthy classes. Instead, it is a diverse group made up of middle class working professionals from many walks of life. Most are refugees; they have clearly come for political reasons. While the economic crunch has made it difficult for many professionals to earn a living, political terrorism has also made it dangerous for them to practice their professions. Teachers, accountants, doctors, reporters, anthropologists, priests, artists, union organizers, other professionals—all belong structurally to what one of my informants termed "the liberal professions." Since 1978, these liberal professions have been targeted by the death squads in coordination with the formal military and police organizations. The death squads have been allowed to murder anyone in Guatemala who shows evidence of leadership ability. Shelton Davis and Julie Hudson of the Anthropology Resource Center in Boston are authors of a report detailing human rights testimony given by 250 Guatemalan exiles (Davis and Hudson 1982). These individuals corroborate that professionals are still targets of assassination. Not only is any form of leadership being destroyed; members of any organization (especially Catholic groups, but even including groups such as Alcoholics Anonymous) are in danger and have been killed as well.

Middle-class people who are refugees are faced with the same privations as the poorer migrants and refugees. In addition, they suffer a downward mobility of social and economic status; this is a great blow to their self-esteem. One example was that of a doctor who had treated a *guerillero* who had come down from the mountains after being shot. Later, the doctor's physician-partner was found machine-gunned to death. The doctor's family prevailed upon him to flee to the United States. Now he is living in the San Francisco Bay Area and, to his dismay, is working as a nursing assistant.

Under such circumstances of flight, new arrivals in the San Francisco Bay Area from both streams of immigrants often feel conflicting emotions about the home they left behind. Guatemalans left behind generally do not approve of the emigrants. They see them as soldiers would see deserters in wartime. (They may be envious.) They describe emigrants as "dumb" because they believe the United States is a paradise, "lazy" because they want life to be easy, and "cowardly" because they do not stay and build Guatemala—still much in ruins from the 1976 earthquake—to what it should be. Immigrants are sensitive to these sentiments and often put off leaving until family tension, nervousness, fear, and anxiety erupt in an internal family crisis; or an incident may occur like the one the doctor experienced. Even so, those who come may claim to be doing so at the behest of others. In the case of the doctor who treated the *guerillero*, he finally came "because his mother insisted that he do so."

Cultural Identity and the Guatemalan Family and Adolescent in the United States

A number of individuals in the Guatemalan network offered observations on what they thought were "cultural characteristics" of Guatemalans. Generally, people said that Guatemalans are a reserved, shy, and quiet people, somewhat given to solemnity and a sense of "holding back." Indians, in particular, are reputed to be "well mannered"; the elites, "social, diplomatic, and outgoing"; and Guatemalans of all classes, *bien educados* (well educated), polite, and respectful of others. One informant told me that the *chapines,* an affectionate slang term for Guatemalans, are humble because they have been more brutalized in Latin American history than many other Latinos. There is an acknowledged pride in the Hispanic heritage that is considered to be more refined and less diluted in Guatemala. At the same time, there is also a great sense of pride in the Mayan heritage; the image is one of great scholars, not warriors. All the pride tends to confer a patriotic dignity to many Guatemalans. On the negative side, some informants (who were Guatemalans themselves) referred to Guatemalans as extremely prejudiced people, particularly regarding race and class. Some also saw Guatemalans as cold, unfriendly, ungenerous, and *tacaño* ("tight," or miserly with both money and friendship). Caution in social relations is the accepted norm, according to most of my informants. As one of my Guatemalan informants put it, "We will be friendly if there's a good reason to be."

Guatemalans are rather critical of other Latinos. Many categorically look down on Mexicans, Salvadorans, and Nicaraguans. There is a racist notion that Mexicans are not as well educated, that they speak vulgarly, and that their Spanish is tainted with Mexicanisms. There is also some historical antipathy to Mexico; they say that Mexico stole the states of Chiapas and Tabasco from what used to be Guatemala. Therefore, Mexicans cannot be trusted. They will smile to your face and stab you in the back. Similarly, several Guatemalan informants told me that Guatemalans think Salvadorans are low class, speak poorly, and are robbers. Nicaraguans are too outspoken and loud, say many Guatemalans. Americans are disparaged as well. They are too arrogant, permissive, lazy, disrespectful, and snobby. Gringa women are presumed to be sexually promiscuous, and gringo men are exploiters. But Americans have the advantage of wealth, and for this they are envied.

In addition to these cultural stereotypes, Guatemalan families bring to the United States an overwhelming sense of suspicion and a reality-based cultural paranoia toward anyone outside the immediate family. This fear and suspicion may be somewhat related to national cultural identity, but it is more likely to spring from the migration process itself and a life filled with economic crises and political intimidation.

A number of my informants stressed to me that these cultural stereotypes are baggage brought from home by older immigrants. They say that the younger Guatemalan immigrants do not have the same prejudices as their parents. "The youth are united." Evidence in the schools, however, of groupings of *cholos* versus those rejecting the *cholo* style indicates that many Guatemalan youth are forced to make identity choices rather quickly once they enter high school. Socioeconomic status here in the new community (not of origin), amount of parental control, and the youth's loyalty to Guatemalan struggles and values as opposed to identification and loyalty to the new American values are some of the factors that informants told me predispose some youth to "go *cholo*" and others to reject the Latino-American subculture. (The *cholo* identity is that of a certain dress code: black pants for boys, hair slicked back, and lots of makeup for girls. There is a tough, street-wise pose and walk, and Chicano English is spoken.) One informant stated that many Guatemalan youth develop a *cholo* identity strictly out of fear.

In some schools, it is practically essential for survival. Students put on a false front. They become superficially Americanized, but it's not really deep. Many of them come from humble backgrounds. They react with "power" to cover their fear. They won't tell you this; they won't admit their past due to *vergüenza* (shame). Embarrassed about their poor English, they react with false pride and violence.

For newly settled Guatemalan families, there are new fears and worries. If the family is separated, as many are, concern is felt for those left behind. If the family is here illegally, everyone is afraid of the possibility of being picked up and deported by *la migra*. In the new neighborhoods, Guatemalans eye American Blacks suspiciously and the gays even more suspiciously. The homosexual lifestyle and, now, AIDS is greatly feared by many Guatemalan immigrants. At a time when migrant families are feeling the precariousness of their cultural identity, a perceived assault on their sexual identity as men and women is another big adjustment they must make. For many of these reasons, people may be afraid to leave their homes and may hesitate to use hospitals and clinics, get drivers' licenses, or attend adult English classes at night.

Because of these and other concerns, most Guatemalan migrants are survival-oriented. For protection, the psychic numbing process goes into operation. People put up blinders. Somatic symptoms are widespread. Clinic personnel recognize common complaints of headaches, low back pain, colds, and (most commonly) insomnia as stress disorders brought to them by Guatemalan patients. Although there may be a small amount of malnutrition and a lot of parasites and dental problems, the most widespread problems are psychosomatic and stress-related.

One young man, here on a legal visa, was studying to be a priest and then was to return to Guatemala. The prospects were obviously quite upsetting to him. I met him through a Catholic church in the area. The day I was planning to interview him, he arrived about an hour late. He told me that he had had an asthma attack that morning and had gone to San Francisco General Hospital. Although he was adamant about continuing the interview, his symptom was suggestive of his anxiety in speaking to me about an emotionally loaded topic, as well as a warning to me to go slow in my questioning of him. When I asked him about the future of Guatemala, he said, "I don't think of tomorrow. I don't know if we're going to wake up tomorrow." While this statement could be analyzed in terms of value orientation, both religious and cultural, in context, it seemed more the statement of a young man who knows at some level that he may be an assassination target. Later I asked him if he had heard of incidents of violence directed toward priests and catechists. He answered, "I don't want to know such things. If I hear them, I will forget them."

For those Guatemalans who stay, the new environment inevitably brings changes in family life. The biggest change is the language. Young people tend to learn English, and parents often do not. Parent-child communication is then difficult, and a language barrier arises within the family. There is a shift in family values to American-style pragmatism, individualism, and, consequently, more conflicts between the generations. Some parents throw all their energy into working; some consciously work to teach their values and language to their children; and some join peer group clubs and/or church activities. There are two Guatemalan clubs, the Club Cultural Guatemalteco and Club Deportivo. One is a social, party-oriented group of Guatemalan expatriates; the other is basically an umbrella organization of Bay Area Guatemalan soccer teams. Usually, though, there is not much time for fun. People work hard and are tired much of the time. Casualties of a life of struggle occur when rewards are thin; then there is isolation, divorce, alcoholism, child abuse, and the other social ills that attach to alienation and lack of mobility.

The families of this San Francisco Bay Area community continue to send their courageous and resourceful youth out into unfamiliar and treacherous terrain; they have survived other struggles before. It is up to them and also to us to help provide a place for the youth (symbolized by the proud and independent quetzal) to come home to rest.

Appendix 2
METHODS OF STUDY

The purpose of this research project was to explore the effect of migration to an urban area of the United States on Guatemalan families, and to determine how families with adolescent members cope with the adjustments that must be made.

This study addressed the following questions:

1. What are the origins of these migrant families, and how have their family histories shaped their present identities? Why did the families decide to emigrate to the United States? What were the conditions of the journey and settling-in process?

2. What are the migrant family cultures/identities and normative rules of behavior at this stage in the family life cycle (having one or more adolescent children)?

3. How do these families accommodate their expectations and rules to the conditions of a new environment? What coping styles do they use? Under what circumstances do families and adolescents pull together to present a cohesive front, and under what circumstances is the adolescent an independent, autonomous entity in the family?

4. To what extent do these families maintain ties and networks with extended family and communities left behind? How does the adolescent family member relate to these ties? What networks are used in the new setting?

This study maps the migration experience for certain Guatemalan families or portions of families (N = 6) who have adolescent children ranging from pubescent twelve-year-olds to nineteen-year-old young men and women. These families are recent arrivals to the San Francisco Bay Area; all have been affected by the increased violence and sociopolitical tension as well as the economic crisis currently gripping Central

America. All of the adolescents and many other family members were interviewed within three years or less of their arrival from Guatemala. Aside from these basic similarities, the families are different from each other in many ways (e.g., in size, composition, amount of fragmentation or geographical dispersion of family members, length of residence in the United States, legal status, political-religious affiliation, socioeconomic status, educational background). Three of the families have at least one adolescent girl, and three have at least one adolescent boy. Most families have more than one adolescent in the household. Altogether there are eleven adolescents represented among the six families, five girls and six boys.

During the initial period of research from 1980-1982, I developed a small urban ethnography through contacts with a number of key informants known to be familiar with the conditions for Central American immigrants and refugees in the urban area under study. I also made a brief reconnaissance trip to Guatemala. This ethnographic material provided important demographic, historical, and structural background regarding the study population. It also helped me locate my study population in some ways (see Appendix 1).

Families who were identified as fulfilling the necessary criteria and who agreed to participate in the study were interviewed by me in Spanish. The interviews were (sound) tape-recorded. Approximately seven interviews (with some variation depending on the family) using semi-structured questionnaires and two standardized family evaluation scales were conducted with each family. (One family declined to participate in the paper-and-pencil testing portion of the study.) Individual interviews were also conducted with each family member aged 12 and over wherever possible. The first three to four interviews elicited data on origins and family history, the migration itself, and acculturation issues. Subsequent interviews explored normative family rules regarding adolescence and adaptive coping strategies. Family social environment and incongruity of perception among family members were scaled by means of a standardized measure, the Family Environment Scale (FES); this test has been developed by Moos and Moos (1976). The standardized Family Adaptability and Cohesion Scale (FACES II) measured the discrepancy family members saw between perceived and ideal family cohesion and perceived and ideal family adaptation. This instrument is Olson's work; it has been refined a number of times since I administered it (Olson et al. 1979; 1983a; 1983b; Flores and Sprenkle 1989; Olson 1989; Touliatos et al. 1989). The two tests were administered to each family (except for the one family that refused); pseudonyms were used in reporting the data.

THE FAMILY ENVIRONMENT SCALE (FES)

This scale of family social environments is based on a typology that is designed for use with "normal," or nonclinical, families. The instrument is widely used, and its reliability and validity have recently been reviewed (Moos 1990). It attempts to describe and measure family environments with respect to interpersonal relationships, personal growth, and organizational structure. It was originally created with a sample of 100 families (including an "ethnic minority" sample); it measures 10 dimensions of family social environment. The ten dimensions are (1) cohesion, (2) expressiveness, and (3) conflict (the interpersonal dimensions); (4) independence, (5) achievement orientation, (6) intellectual-cultural orientation, (7) active-recreational orientation, and (8) moral-religious emphasis (the personal growth dimensions); (9) organization and (10) control (the organizational dimensions).

The dimensions are measured by having all family members over the age of nine respond to a 90-item true-false questionnaire (in Spanish and back translated into English) on various aspects of their family environments. Scores are averaged to obtain a family profile. The amount of disagreement between family members' scores within each family is totaled and divided by the number of respondents to obtain a family incongruence score for each family.

In Moos' sample, there are six family clusters: expression-oriented, structure-oriented, independence-oriented, achievement-oriented, moral/religious-oriented, and conflict-oriented; the standard family incongruence score is 16. Ethnic minority families are commonly found in the structure-oriented and achievement-oriented clusters; they are less often represented in the expression-oriented and moral/religious-oriented clusters (Moos and Moos 1976). I tested the Guatemalan families in my study with this scale to see what family cultural styles of coping emerge.

FAMILY ADAPTABILITY AND COHESION SCALE (FACES)

In reviewing a number of concepts from the family therapy and social science fields, two significant dimensions of family behavior emerge: cohesion and adaptability. These dimensions are commonly regarded to by theorists and clinicians as significant in evaluating the success of families in coping with the exigencies of life. They have been used by family therapists in developing and refining a "circumplex model of marital and family systems" (Olson et al. 1979; 1983a). Investigations are continuing as to the methodological usefulness and applicability of

Olson's construct and instrument in a variety of clinical and research applications (Flores and Sprenkle 1989; Grotevant 1989; Olson 1989; Touliatos et al. 1989; Anderson and Gavazzi 1990; Green et al. 1991).

In Olson's model, cohesion is defined as "the emotional bonding that family members have toward one another" (Olson et al. 1983a). The functioning hypothesis is that of four levels of cohesion ranging from disengaged to separated to connected to finally, enmeshed. The middle two levels (separated and connected) make for optimal family functioning. The two extremes (disengaged and enmeshed) are usually seen as problematic.

Adaptability is the second dimension in Olson's circumplex model. It is defined as "the ability of a family system to change its power structure, role relationships, and relationship rules in response to situational and developmental stress" (Olson et al. 1983a). As with cohesion, the hypothesis works from four levels of adaptability (from rigid to structured to flexible to chaotic). Here, too, the middle two levels (structured and flexible) make for optimal family functioning; the extremes are said to be more dysfunctional.

Olson's FACES II test[1] measures the dimensions of cohesion and adaptability in families by having all family members over the age of nine respond to a 30-item questionnaire (in Spanish and back translated into English) in which they rank various features and assumptions about family life that pertain to cohesion and adaptability. Ranking ranges from "never" to "always" with three in-between choices. Each family member's perceived family cohesion and adaptability is scaled, as well as each family member's notion of ideal family cohesion and adaptability. For each individual, the direction of the arrow indicates the desired goal; the point of origin of the arrow indicates the perceived condition of the family. How well the ideal corresponds with the perceived real levels of cohesion and adaptation can then be analyzed, as well as the correspondence between the desires and direction of the arrows of the various family members.

One of Olson's recent refinements focuses on the discrepancy between perceived and ideal scores (i.e., satisfaction) as the most important feature of the test in terms of successful family functioning. Accordingly, it is possible to get a rough idea of how successfully a family is functioning based on its members' own emic perception. To do this, the point difference in scores for all family members within each family is totaled and divided by the number of respondents to obtain a family discrepancy score for each family. Although to date there is no standard score of what constitutes successful versus unsuccessful family functioning, it seems that families with higher discrepancy scores are less successful at meeting their own self-defined needs than those with lower scores. This assessment of satisfaction among the various family members may be the key to successful family functioning over and above "balanced" cohesion and adaptability. That is, how family members feel about the kind of family they have (discrepancy between perceived and ideal scores) is more important than what type of family system they have. Olson has thus opened up the model up to varying functional cultural styles (Olson et al. 1983a).

NOTES

CHAPTER 1

1. The anthropological definition of family is "married couple or other adult kinsfolk who cooperate economically and in the upbringing of children, and all or most of whom share a common dwelling" (Gough 1971, p. 760).

2. This respect often has a decidedly ambivalent quality due to the history of conquest that is the Latin American legacy (Adams 1970).

3. *Cholo* identity comes from adolescent pan–Latin American subculture. It is characterized by a certain style of dress, use of slang, and gang–related recreational activities such as low-riding, marijuana smoking, and so forth.

4. "Compartmentalize" is a psychological term referring to the isolation and blocking up of ideas, feelings, values, attitudes, and behaviors rather than permitting their consistency and integration in the personality (Chaplin 1968; p. 95).

CHAPTER 2

1. Much of the migration is seasonal and related to labor; many Mexicans consider the neighboring southwestern portion of the United States to be historically their birthright, stolen by a deceiving U.S. government in the Treaty of Guadalupe Hidalgo of 1848. Therefore, they are not really migrating, and they remain, after all, Mexicans (McWilliams 1949; Wiest 1979).

2. *Cuello* means influence, or "pull."

3. The total family score was above 60 percent in the area of achievement—their highest score. Their other two above-average scores were in moral-religious emphasis and in conflict (both above 55 percent). The dotted line on the Family Environment Scale denotes the standardized or normative scores of Moos and Moos' sample families. Any deviation from normative scores suggests idiosyncratic family cultural styles and environments that play up certain features and play down others to varying degrees (see Appendix 2).

4. The scores in the FACES test fall into the "rigid" (adaptation type) and "disengaged" (cohesion type) rectangle; all family members perceive their family (through self-report) to be rigidly disengaged (see Appendix 2 for a discussion of the FACES test). At the same time, the direction of the arrows describes the

trajectory of individual family members' wishes and desires—their family "ideal." The two arrows for Éster, the mother, and Laura, the adolescent, end in the "chaotic" (adaptation type) and "separated" (cohesion type) rectangle. These arrows indicate dissatisfaction on their parts with the family as they see it; the arrows also indicate what they would like to see instead. Inclusion of a number of family members' reports offers the reader an opportunity to compare and contrast the perceived and ideal visions of the family from the points of view of its various members.

5. Historically, the overt exercise of leadership was taken on by a *caudillo* who often became a tyrant. Power in Guatemala is still tainted. It tends to be ephemeral, and the leader is overthrown by some sort of coup or deception. Thus, overt leadership is by definition a dangerous social role (see Asturias 1973).

6. *Mojado* is a slang term for undocumented migrant, literally a "wetback" from crossing the Rio Grande River.

7. Ms. Navarro speaks fluent Kekchí, the language of the Alta Verapaz region. She says she was raised by Kekchí Indians. She says also that the Kekchí language, customs, dress, and manners are superior to other Indian groups. She owns a Kekchí blouse and skirt, which she wears on special occasions.

8. The godmother of Mrs. Castillo's child is *comadre* to Mrs. Castillo, an example of a fictive kin relationship at the same generational level.

9. Moos reports the average incongruence score for families on the Family Environment Scale (FES) to be 16 (Moos and Moos 1976).

CHAPTER 3

1. Federal law mandates that all children are eligible for public education up to age 18. After age 18, most colleges provide federally sponsored loan programs for which undocumented students are ineligible.

2. There is internal disagreement in the other two families in the study, but to a lesser degree.

3. The finding suggests that the youth in this study have some longing for supportive and nurturant family life that they have never experienced or that they missed while they were separated from their parents.

4. The Chavez family was not tested.

5. Although these two families do show mild internal disagreement over the direction they would like to see their families take vis-à-vis cohesion and adaptation (more or less), the average discrepancy scores between ideal and perceived cohesion and adaptation range from only 2.5 to 6.5.

6. *Machismo* is sexually aggressive, arrogant, hypersensitive male behavior. In its culturally congruent state, the true *macho* is protector and provider. He also is expressive of strong feelings (the expression *llorar como un macho* means "to cry like a man").

7. *Marianismo* is self-sacrificing female behavior that courts admiration. In its culturally congruent state, the female is the moral leader of the household.

8. *Deshecharse* means to ventilate.

APPENDIX 1

1. Reports from 1984 are that bribes of $700 per person are also part of the process.

APPENDIX 2

1. Three versions of the FACES test are now available, FACES I, II, and III. FACES IV will be available soon.

BIBLIOGRAPHY

Adams, Richard N. 1967. *The Second Sowing: Power and Secondary Development in Latin America.* San Francisco: Chandler Publishing Co.

———. 1970. *Crucifixion by Power: Essays on Guatemalan National Structure 1944-1966.* Austin: University of Texas Press.

American Psychiatric Association. 1987. *Diagnostic and Statistical Manual of Mental Disorders.* 3d ed. rev. Washington, D.C.: APA.

Anderson, Stephen, and Gavazzi, Stephen. 1990. "A Test of the Olson Circumplex Model: Examining Its Curvilinear Assumption and the Presence of Extreme Types." *Family Process* 29(3).

Angell, R. 1936. *The Family Encounters the Depression.* New York: Charles Scribner's Sons.

Antonovsky, Aaron. 1971. "Social and Cultural Factors in CHD: An Israel-North American Sibling Study." *Israel Journal of Medical Sciences* 7(12).

Aponte, Harry. 1976. "Underorganization in the Poor Family." In *Family Therapy: Theory and Practice,* edited by Philip Guerin. New York: Gardner Press.

Argüello, David. 1990. Personal communication.

Arizpe, Lourdes. 1975. *Indígenas en la Ciudad de México: El Caso de Las Marías.* México, D.F.: México Sep Setenas.

Aron, Adrienne. 1986. Psychological Problems of Salvadoran Refugees in California. Paper presented at symposium, Psychological Effects of Forced Relocation: An International Perspective. Ninety–fourth annual convention of the American Psychological Association, Washington, D.C.

Aronowitz, Michael. 1984. "The Social and Emotional Adjustment of Immigrant Children: A Review of the Literature." *International Migration Review* 18(2).

Arroyo, William, and Eth, Spencer. 1985. "Children Traumatized by Central American Warfare." In *Post-Traumatic Stress in Children,* edited by

Spencer Eth and Robert Pynoos.   Washington, D.C.: American
    Psychiatric Press.
Asturias, Miguel Angel. 1973. *El Señor Presidente*. San Jose, Costa Rica:
    Editorial Universitaria Centroamericano.
Bach, Robert L., and Schraml, Lisa. 1982. "Migration, Crisis and Theoretical
    Conflict." *International Migration Review* 16(2).
Balgopal, Pallassana. 1988. "Social Networks and Asian Indian Families." In
    Ethnicity and Race: Critical Concepts in Social Work, edited by Carolyn
    Jacobs and Dorcas Bowles. Silver Springs, MD.: National Association
    of Social Workers.
Baucic, J. 1976. *Treatises on Migration*, vol. 24. Zagreb: Center for Migration
    Research.
Bernal, Guillermo, and Flores-Ortiz, Yvette.   1982.   "Latino Families in
    Therapy: Engagement and Evaluation." *Journal of Marital and Family
    Therapy* 8(3).
Bernard, Viola, et al.   1965.   "Dehumanization: A Composite Psychological
    Defense in Relation to Modern War." In *Stress and Coping, An
    Anthology.* edited by R. Lazarus and A. Monat. New York: Columbia
    University Press.
Berry, J. W., et al.   1987.   "Comparative Studies of Acculturative Stress."
    International Migration Review 21(3).
Boehlein, J. K.   1987.   "Clinical Relevance of Grief and Mourning among
    Cambodian Refugees." *Social Science and Medicine* 25(7).
Bourne, P. 1975. "The Chinese Student—Acculturation and Mental Illness."
    Psychiatry 38(3).
Bowen, Murray.   1978.   *Family Therapy in Clinical Practice*.   New York:
    Jason Aronson.
Boyd, Monica.   1989.   "Family and Personal Networks in International
    Migration: Recent Developments and New Agendas." *International
    Migration Review* 23(3).
Brintnall, Douglas. 1979a. "Race Relations in the Southeastern Highlands of
    Mesoamerica." *American Ethnologist* 6(4).
———.   1979b.   *Revolt against the Dead: Race Relations in the Southeast
    Highlands of Mesoamerica*. New York: Gordon and Breach.
Brody, E. 1969. *Behavior in New Environments: Adaptation of Immigrant
    Populations*. Beverly Hills, Calif.: Sage.
Burawoy, M.   1976.   "The Functions and Reproduction of Migrant Labor:
    Comparative Material from Southern Africa and the United States."
    American Journal of Sociology 8(5).
Burnam, M., et al. 1987. "Acculturation and Lifetime Prevalence of Psychiatric
    Disorders among Mexican Americans in Los Angeles." *Journal of
    Health and Social Behavior* 28.
Burnett, Virginia.   1986.   A History of Protestantism in Guatemala. Ph.D.
    diss., Tulane University, New Orleans.
Carter, Betty, and McGoldrick, Monica, eds. 1988. *The Changing Family Life
    Cycle*. New York: Gardner Press.

Chaplin, J. P. 1968. *Dictionary of Psychology*. New York: Dell.

Clark, Margaret, et al. 1976. "Explorations of Acculturation: Towards a Model of Ethnic Identity." *Human Organization*. 35(3).

Cohen, Lucy. 1979. *Culture, Disease and Stress Among Latino Immigrants*. Washington, D.C.: The Catholic University of America.

Cohen, Lucy M., and Fernandez, C. L. 1974. "Ethnic Identity and Psychocultural Adaptation of Spanish-Speaking Families." *Child Welfare* 53(7).

Cohler, B. J., and Lieberman, M. A. 1980. "Social Relations and Mental Health: Middle Aged and Older Men and Women from Three European Ethnic Groups." *Research on Aging* 2(4).

Daniels, Roger. 1990. *Coming to America: A History of Immigration in American Life*. New York: Harper Collins Publishers.

Davis, Kingsley. 1940. "The Sociology of Parent-Youth Conflict." *American Sociological* Review 5(1).

Davis, Shelton. 1983. Social Effects of Political Violence in Guatemala. Lecture given at Center for Latin American Studies. Berkeley, Calif., April 27.

Davis, Shelton H., and Hudson, Julie. 1982. *Witness to Political Violence in Guatemala*. Boston: Oxfam America.

Durham, William. 1977. *Scarcity and Survival in Central America: Ecological Origins of the Soccer War*. Stanford: Stanford University Press.

Early, John. 1982. *The Demographic Structure and Evolution of a Peasant System: The Guatemalan Population*. Boca Raton: University Presses of Florida.

Eckholm, Erik. 1984. "The Human Hand in Natural Disasters." *San Francisco Chronicle*, This World Section (September 9): 16.

Episcopado Guatemalteco. 1988. *El Clamor por la Tierra: Carta Pastoral Nueva Guatemala de la Asunción*. Guatemala, CA.

Ehrlich, Paul, et al. 1979. *The Golden Door: International Migration, Mexico and the United States*. New York: Balantine Books.

Erikson, Eric. 1954. "Growth and Crisis in the Healthy Personality." In *Personality in Nature, Society, and Culture*, edited by C. Kluckhohn and H. A. Murray. London: J. Cape.

Fainstein, Susan, and Fainstein, Norman. 1989. "The Racial Dimension in Urban Political Economy." *Urban Affairs Quarterly* 25(2).

Falicov, Celia. 1988a. *Family Transitions: Continuity and Change over the Life Cycle*. New York: Guilford Press.

———. 1988b. Presentation to Bicultural Association of Spanish-speaking Therapists and Advocates. Alameda: California School of Professional Psychology, October.

Falicov, Celia J., and Karrer, Betty M. 1980. "Cultural Variations in the Family Life Cycle: The Mexican-American Family." In *The Family Life Cycle: A Framwork for Family Therapy*, edited by Betty Carter and Monica McGoldrick. New York: Gardner Press.

Faris, R. E., and Dunham, H. W. 1939. *Mental Disorders in Urban Areas: An Ecological Study of Schizophrenia and Other Psychoses*. Chicago:

University of Chicago Press.

Ferguson, Barbara. 1984. Successful Refugee Resettlement: Vietnamese Values, Beliefs, and Strategies. Ph.D. diss., University of California, Berkeley.

Ferguson, Dolores. 1984. Personal communication.

Ferris, Elizabeth. 1987. *The Central American Refugees.* New York: Praeger Publishers.

Figley, Charles. 1989. *Helping Traumatized Families.* San Francisco: Jossey Bass.

Flores, M. T., and Sprenkle, D. H. 1989. "Can Therapists Use FACES III with Mexican-Americans? A Preliminary Analysis." In *Circumplex Model: Systematic Assessment and Treatment of Families,* edited by David Olson et al. New York: Haworth Press.

Freeman, James. 1989. *Hearts of Sorrow: Vietnamese-American Lives.* Stanford: Stanford University Press.

Fried, Jonathan L., et al. 1983. *Guatemala in Rebellion: Unfinished History.* New York: Grove Press.

Fuentes, Carlos. 1981. "Farewell, Monroe Doctrine." *Harper's,* August, 263.

Geertz, Clifford. 1973. *The Interpretation of Cultures: Selected Essays.* New York: Basic Books.

Golden, R., and McConnell, M., eds. 1986. *Sanctuary: The New Underground Railroad.* New York: Maryknoll Orbis Books.

Goody, Jack. 1958. *The Developmental Cycle of Domestic Group*s. London: Cambridge University Press.

Gordon, A. J. 1978. "Hispanic Drinking after Migration: The Case of Dominicans. *Medical Anthropology* 2(4).

Gough, Kathleen. 1971. "The Origin of the Family." *Journal of Marriage and the Family.* 33(4).

Graves, T. D. 1967. "Acculturation, Access and Alcohol in a Tri-Ethnic Community." *American Anthropologist* 69(3-4).

Green, Robert G., et al. 1991. "Evaluating FACES III and the Circumplex Model: 2,440 Families." *Family Process* 30(1).

Grotevant, Harold D. 1989. "Theory in Guiding Family Assessment." *Journal of Family Psychology* 3(2).

Guillet, D., and Uzzell, D., eds. 1976. *New Approaches to the Study of Migration.* Houston, Tex.: Rice University Press.

Gutierrez, José. 1984. Personal communication.

Hansen, Marcus. 1952. "The Third Generation in America." *Commentary* 14.

Harbison, S. F. 1981. "Family Structure and Family Strategy in Migration Decision Making." In *Migration Decision Making: Multidisciplinary Approaches to Macrolevel Studies in Developed and Developing Countries,* edited by S. F. DeJong and R. W. Gardner. New York: Pergamon Press.

Helms, Mary. 1975. *Middle America: A Culture History of Heartland and Frontiers.* Englewood Cliffs, N.J.: Prentice Hall.

Hill, Reuben. 1949. *Families under Stress*. New York: Harper Social Science Series.
Hollingshead, A., and Redlich, F. 1958. *Social Class and Mental Illness: A Community Study*. New York: Wiley and Sons.
Howard, A. 1974. *Ain't No Big Thing: Coping Strategies in a Hawaiian American Community*. Honolulu: University of Hawaii Press.
Howard, George. 1991. "Culture Tales: A Narrative Approach to Thinking, Cross-Cultural Psychology and Psychotherapy." *American Psychologist* 46(3).
Hull, Diana. 1979. "Migration, Adaptation and Illness: A Review." *Social Science and Medicine* 13.
Immerman, Richard H. 1982. *The CIA in Guatemala*. Austin: University of Texas Press.
Jacob, Jeffrey. 1980. "Urban Poverty Children and the Consumption of Popular Culture: A Perspective on Marginality Theses from a Latin American Squatter Settlement." *Human Organization* 39(3).
Keefe, Susan, et al. 1979. "The Mexican-American Extended Family as an Emotional Support System." *Human Organization* 38(2).
Kinzer, Stephen, and Schlesinger, Stephen. 1981. *Bitter Fruit*. Garden City, N.Y.: Doubleday and Company.
Kunz, E. F. 1981. "Exile and Resettlement: Refugee Theory." *International Migration Review* 15(1-2).
Kuo, W. H., and Tsai, Y. 1986. "Social Networking, Hardiness, and Immigrant Mental Health." *Journal of Health and Social Behavior* 27.
Leighton, Dorothea, et al. 1963. *The Character of Danger*. New York: Basic Books.
Lewis, Oscar. 1959. *Five Families*. New York: Basic Books.
———. 1961. *The Children of Sanchez*. New York: Random House.
———. 1966. *La Vida: A Puerto Rican Family in the Culture of Poverty, San Juan and New York*. New York: Random House.
Lifton, Robert Jay. 1967. *Death in Life*. New York: Random House.
Lomnitz, Larissa Adler. 1977. *Networks and Marginality: Life in a Mexican Shantytown*. New York: Academic Press.
McCubbin, Hamilton, and Figley, Charles. 1983. "Bridging Normative and Catastrophic Family Stress." In *Stress and the Family: Coping with Normative Transitions*, vol. 1, edited by H. McCubbin and C. Figley. New York: Brunner/Mazel.
McCubbin, Hamilton, et al. 1980. "Family Stress and Coping: A Decade Review." *Journal of Marriage and the Family* 42(4).
MacLeod, Murdo J. 1973. *Spanish Central America: A Socioeconomic History from 1520-1720*. Berkeley: University of California Press.
McWilliams, Carey. 1949. *North from Mexico*. Philadelphia: J.B. Lippincott Co.
Madanes, Chloe. 1981. *Strategic Family Therapy*. San Francisco: Jossey Bass.
Maduro, Renaldo, and Martinez, Carlos. 1979. "Latino Dream Analysis: Opportunity for Self and Social Confrontation." *Social Casework*

55(8).

Manz, Beatriz.   1988.   *Refugees of a Hidden War.*   New York: SUNY Press.

Martin-Baró, Ignacio.   1988.   Political Violence and War as Causes of Psycho-
    social Trauma in El Salvador.   Address presented at symposium,
    Central American Immigrants and Refugees.   San Francisco State
    University, March 10.

Martinez Palaez, Severo.   1976.   *La Patria del Criollo.*   San José, Costa Rica:
    Editorial Universitaria.

Massey, D. S., and Schnabel, K. M.   1983.   "Recent Trends in Hispanic Im-
    migration to the United States." *International Migration Review* 17(2).

Menchú, Rigoberta.   1990.   "Cry for Justice."   *New World Times* 2(1) (San
    Francisco), Winter.

Moors, Marilyn.   1988.   "Indian Labor and the Guatemalan Crisis: Evidence
    from History and Anthropology."   In *Central American Historical
    Perspectives on the Continuing Crisis*, edited by Ralph Woodward.
    Westport, Conn.: Greenwood Press.

Moos, R.   1990.   "Conceptual and Empirical Approaches to Developing
    Family-Based Assessment Procedures: Resolving the Case of the Family
    Environment Scale." *Family Process* 29(2).

Moos, R., and Moos, B.   1976.   "A Typology of Family Social Environ-
    ments." *Family Process* 15(4).

Muller, R. M.   1976.   *School Children under Stress.*   New York: S. Karger
    Bale.

Muñoz, L.   1980.   "Exile as Bereavement: Socio-Psychological Manifestations
    of Chilean Exiles in Great Britain."   *British Journal of Medical
    Psychology* 53.

Murguía, Edward.   1975.   *Assimilation, Colonialism, and the Mexican-American
    People.*   Austin: Center for Mexican American Studies Monograph no.
    1, University of Texas.

Murphy, H. B.   1977.   "Migration, Culture and Mental Health." *Psychological
    Medicine* 7(4).

Olson, David.   1989.   "Circumplex Model of Family Systems VIII: Family
    Assessment and Intervention."   In *Circumplex Model: Systematic
    Assessment and Treatment of Families*, edited by D. H. Olson, et al. New
    York: Haworth Press.

Olson, David, et al.   1979.   "Circumplex Model of Marital and Family Systems:
    1. Cohesion and Adaptability Dimensions, Family Types, and Clinical
    Applications." *Family Process* 18(1).

———.   1983a.   "Circumplex Model of Marital and Family Systems: VI.
    Theoretical Update." *Family Process* 22(1).

———.   1983b. *Families: What Makes Them Work.* Beverly Hills, Calif.: Sage
    Publications.

Padilla, Amado.   1980.   *Acculturation: Theory, Models, and Some New Findings.*
    Boulder, Colo.: Westview Press.

Palacio, Joseph.   1982.   Lecture on Central America and Belize, University of
    California, Berkeley, October.

Paris, Joel. 1978. "The Symbolic Return: Psychodynamic Aspects of Immigration and Exile." *Journal of American Academy of Psychoanalysis* 6(1).

Peñalosa, Fernando. 1986. *Central Americans in Los Angeles.* Los Angeles: Spanish Speaking Mental Health Research Center, UCLA.

Perera, Victor. 1986. *Rites.* New York: Harcourt Brace Jovanovich.

Perlman, Janet. 1976. *The Myth of Marginality—Urban Poverty and Politics in Rio de Janeiro.* Berkeley: University of California Press.

Portes, Alejandro, and Bach, Robert L. 1985. *Latin Journey: Cuban and Mexican Immigrants in the United States.* Berkeley: University of California Press.

Portes, Alejandro, and Borocz, Jozsef. 1989. "Contemporary Immigration: Theoretical Perspectives on Its Determinants and Modes of Incorporation." *International Migration Review* 23(3).

Portes, Alejandro, and Rumbaut, Ruben. 1990. *Immigrant America: A Portrait.* Berkeley: University of California Press.

Redfield, Robert. 1947. "The Folk Society." *American Journal of Sociology* 52(4).

Roberts, Bryan. 1973. *Organizing Strangers: Poor Families in Guatemala City.* Austin: University of Texas Press.

Rogler, Lloyd, et al. 1991. "Acculturation and Mental Health Status among Hispanics: Convergence and New Directions for Research." *American Psychologist* 46(6).

Romano-V, Octavio. 1973. "The Anthropology and Sociology of the Mexican-Americans: The Distortion of Mexican-American History." In *Voices: Readings from El Grito*, edited by Octavio Romano-V. Berkeley, Calif.: Quinto Sol Publications.

Rumbaut, Ruben. 1989. "Portraits, Patterns and Predictors of the Refugee Adaptation Process." In *Refugees as Immigrants: Cambodians, Laotians, and Vietnamese in America*, edited by David Haines. Totowa, N.J.: Rowman and Littlefield.

Salcido, Ramón. 1979. "Undocumented Aliens." *Social Work* 24(4).

Salgado de Snyder, Nelly, et al. 1990. "Migración y Éstres Post-traumático: El Caso de los Mexicanos y Centroamericanos en los Estados Unidos." *Acta Psiquiatra Psicológica América Latina* 36(3-4).

San Francisco Examiner. 1982. "Central America: The Tortured Land." Summer Series-Fifteen Part Report, edited by Scott Winokur.

Sarbin, T. R., ed. 1986. *Narrative Psychology: The Storied Nature of Human Conduct.* New York: Praeger Press.

Sassen-Koob, Saskia. 1984. "Notes on the Incorporation of Third World Women into Wage Labor through Immigration and Off-Shore Production." *International Migration Review* 18(4).

Schreiber, Janet. 1972. "The Decision to Move as a Response to Family Crisis." In *Migration: Report of the Research Conference on Migration*, Rome Publication no. 5. Rome, Italy: U.N. Defence Research Unit.

Schwab, J. J., et al. 1979. *Social Order and Mental Health: The Florida Health*

Study. New York: Brunner/Mazel.

Shisana, O.. and Celentano D. D. 1987. "Relationship of Chronic Stress, Social Support, and Coping Style to Health among Namibian Refugees." *Social Science and Medicine* 24(2).

Sluzki, Carlos. 1973. Acculturation and Conflict in the Latino Family. Paper presented to San Francisco Family Forum, October.

———. 1979. "Migration and Family Conflict." *Family Process* 18(4).

Smith, Carol. 1984. "Local History in a Global Context: Social and Economic Transitions in Western Guatemala." *Comparative Studies in Society and History* 26.

Smith, Carol, and Boyer, Jeff. 1987. "Central America since 1979: Part I." *Annual Review of Anthropology* 16.

Spencer, Scott. 1979. "Childhood's End." *Harper's,* May, 258.

Srole, L., et al. 1962. *Mental Health in the Metropolis: The Midtown Study,* vol. 1. New York: McGraw-Hill.

Steinglass, Peter. 1978. "The Conceptualization of Marriage from a Systems Theory Perspective." In *Marriage and Marital Therapy: Psychoanalytic Behavioral and Systems Theory Perspectives,* edited by T. J. Paulino and B. S. McCrady. New York: Brunner/Mazel.

Stevens, Evelyn. 1973. "Machismo and Marianismo." *Transaction: Social Science and Modern Society* 10(6).

Stierlin, Helm, and Ravenscroft, K. 1972. "Varieties of Adolescent Separation Conflict." *British Journal of Medical Psychology* 45(4).

Suarez-Orozco, Marcelo. 1989. *Central American Refugees and U.S. High Schools: A Psychosocial Study of Motivation and Achievement.* Stanford: Stanford University Press.

Tax, Sol. 1952. *Heritage of Conquest: The Ethnology of Middle America.* Glencoe, Ill.: Free Press.

Tedlock, Dennis, trans. 1985. *Popol Vuh: The Mayan Book of the Dawn of Life.* New York: Simon and Schuster.

Tobias, Peter. 1976. "Explanations of Emigration from Grenada, West Indies." In *New Approaches to the Study of Migration,* edited by D. Guillet and D. Uzzell. Houston, Tex.: Rice University Press.

Touliatos, J., et al. 1989. *Handbook of Family Measurement Techniques.* Newbury Park, Calif.: Sage Publications.

United States Committee for Refugees. 1989. *World Refugee Survey: 1988 in Review.* Washington, D.C.: American Council of Nationalities Service.

van der Kolk, Bessel A. 1987. *Psychological Trauma.* Washington, D.C.: American Psychiatric Association.

Vega, William, et al. 1984. "The Prevalence of Depressive Symptoms Among Mexican-Americans and Anglos." *American Journal of Epidemiology* 120(2).

Vernez, Georges. 1991. "Current Global Refugee Situation and International Public Policy." *American Psychologist* 46(6).

Wallace, Steven. 1986. "Central American and Mexican Immigrant Characteristics and Economic Incorporation in California." *International Migration Review* 20(3).

Walsh, Froma. 1982. "Conceptualizations of Normal Family Functions." In *Normal Family Processes*, edited by F. Walsh. New York: Guilford Press.

Warheit, George J., et al. 1985. "Mexican-American Immigration and Mental Health: A Comparative Analysis of Psychosocial Distress and Dysfunction." In *Stress and Hispanic Mental Health*, edited by William Vega and Manuel Miranda. Rockville, Md.: National Institute of Mental Health.

Warren, Kay B. 1978. *The Symbolism of Subordination: Indian Identity in a Guatemalan Town*. Austin: University of Texas Press.

West, Martin, and Moore, Erin. 1989. "Undocumented Workers in the United States and South Africa: A Comparative Study of Changing Control." *Human Organization* 48(1).

White, R. A. 1984. *The Morass: U.S. Intervention in Central America*. New York: Harper and Row.

Wiest, R. E. 1979. "Anthropological Perspectives on Return Migration: A Critical Commentary." *Papers in Anthropology* 20.

Wolf, Eric. 1959. *Sons of the Shaking Earth*. Chicago: University of Chicago Press.

Wood, Charles. 1982. "Equilibrium and Historical-Structural Perspectives on Migration." *International Migration Review* 16(2).

Zolberg, Aristede R. 1989. "The Next Waves: Migration Theory for a Changing World." *International Migration Review* 23(3).

INDEX

About the Author

NORITA VLACH is a Californian of part-Guatemalan ethnicity who teaches Social Work at San Jose State University. Dr. Vlach has worked as a clinical social worker in Latino communities and as a medical anthropologist studying refugees.

A|